The 1997 McGraw-Hill Training and Performance Sourcebook

Mel Silberman, Editor

Assisted by
Carol Auerbach

McGraw-Hill

New York   San Francisco   Washington, D.C.   Auckland   Bogotá
Caracas   Lisbon   London   Madrid   Mexico City   Milan
Montreal   New Delhi   San Juan   Singapore
Sydney   Tokyo   Toronto

International Standard Serial Number:
The 1997 McGraw-Hill Training and Performance Sourcebook
ISSN 1084-1342

1 2 3 4 5 6 7 8 9 0   EDW/EDW   9 0 1 0 9 8 7 6   (Paperback)
1 2 3 4 5 6 7 8 9 0   EDW/EDW   9 0 1 0 9 8 7 6   (Looseleaf)

ISBN 0-07-057840-0 (Paperback)
PN 0-07-057942-3
PART OF
ISBN 0-07-057841-9 (Looseleaf)

The sponsoring editor for this book was Richard Narramore, the editing supervisor was Fred Dahl, the designer was Inkwell Publishing Services, and the production supervisor was Suzanne W. B. Rapcavage.

Printed and bound by Edwards Brothers.

McGraw-Hill books are available at special quantity discounts to use as premiums and sales promotions, or for use in corporate training programs. For more information, please write to the Director of Special Sales, McGraw-Hill, 11 West 19th Street, New York, NY 10011. Or contact your local bookstore.

CONTENTS

TOPICAL INDEX
Find a Tool for Your Specific Topic

In the place of a traditional index is the following classification by topic of the 40 tools found in *The 1997 McGraw-Hill Training and Performance Sourcebook.*

PREFACE

Welcome to the second year of *The McGraw-Hill Training and Performance Sourcebook,* an annual collection of practical tools to develop human resources. *The 1996 Sourcebook* was a huge success. *The 1997 Sourcebook* has another great lineup of resources for your professional use.

Along with its companion, *The McGraw-Hill Team and Organization Development Sourcebook, The McGraw-Hill Training and Performance Sourcebook* provides the latest cutting-edge advice and learning aids on topics important to today's public and private sector organizations. While *The Team and Organization Development Sourcebook* emphasizes systemwide issues, *The McGraw-Hill Training and Performance Sourcebook* focuses on development and support at the individual level of the organization.

The McGraw-Hill Training and Performance Sourcebook includes discussion of both training and nontraining solutions to performance problems. You will find several materials, prepared by leading experts, that enhance your efforts as a trainer, instructor, or coach. You will also discover ways to support individual performance through such means as mentoring and performance technology.

The 1997 Sourcebook contains 40 training activities, assessment instruments, handouts, and practical guides ... creating a ready-to-use toolkit for trainers, HRD consultants, performance support specialists, and subject matter experts. It is also invaluable for managers and other organizational representatives who are interested in coaching, training, learning, and performance development. Best of all, because these tools are reproducible, they can be shared with others.

Here are some of the topics you will find covered in *The 1997 McGraw-Hill Training and Performance Sourcebook:*

✓ Alternatives to classroom training
✓ Career development
✓ Communication skills
✓ Computer training
✓ Diversity and cross-cultural awareness
✓ Evaluation
✓ Learning and training techniques

✓ Management development
✓ Performance support
✓ Personal effectiveness
✓ Sales
✓ Training design

I hope you will find *The 1997 McGraw-Hill Training and Performance Sourcebook* to be a one-stop resource you can draw on again and again in your efforts to facilitate learning and support performance improvement.

Mel Silberman
Princeton, New Jersey

TRAINING ACTIVITIES

In this section of *The 1997 McGraw-Hill Training and Performance Sourcebook,* you will find fourteen training activities. They are designed to:

✓ Introduce training topics

✓ Practice skills

✓ Promote attitude change

✓ Increase knowledge

✓ Stimulate discussion

✓ Foster participation and retention

✓ Enhance concepts

You can use these activities in a variety of settings:

✓ Classroom-based training sessions

✓ Meetings and retreats

✓ One-to-one coaching

✓ Distance learning

✓ Consultations

All of the activities featured here are highly participatory. They are designed in the belief that learning and change best occur through *experience* and *reflection.* As opposed to preaching or lecturing, experiential activities place people directly within a concrete situation. Typically, participants are asked to solve a problem, complete an assignment, or communicate information. Often, the task can be quite challenging. Sometimes, it can also be a great deal of fun. The bottom line, however, is that participants become active partners in the learning of new concepts or in the development of new ideas.

The experiences contained in the activities you are about to read can also be of two kinds: *simulated* and *real-world.* Although some may find them to be artificial, well-designed simulations can provide an effective analogy to real-world experiences. They also have the advantage of being time-saving shortcuts to longer, drawn-out activities. Sometimes, of course, there is no substitute for real-world experience. Activities that engage teams in actual, ongoing work can serve as a powerful mechanism for change.

Experience, by itself, is not always "the best teacher." Reflecting on the experience, however, can yield wisdom and insight. You will find that the training activities in this section contain helpful guidelines for reflection. Expect a generous selection of questions to process or debrief the actual activities.

All the activities have been written for ease of use. A concise overview of each activity is provided. You will be guided, step by step, through the activity instructions. All the necessary participant materials are included. For your photocopying convenience, these materials are on separate pages. Any materials you need to prepare in advance have been kept to a minimum. Special equipment or physical arrangements are seldom needed.

Best of all, the activities are designed so that you can easily modify or customize them to your specific requirements. Also, time allocations are readily adaptable. Furthermore, many of the activities are "frame exercises" … generic activities that can be used for many topics or subject matters. You will find it easy to plug in the content relevant to your team's circumstances.

As you conduct any of these activities, bear in mind that experiential activity is especially successful if you do a good job as facilitator. Here are some common mistakes people make in facilitating experiential activities:

1. *Motivation:* Participants aren't invited to buy into the activity themselves or sold the benefits of joining in. Participants don't know what to expect during the exercise.

2. *Directions:* Instructions are lengthy and unclear. Participants cannot visualize what the facilitator expects from them.

3. *Group Process:* Subgroups are not composed effectively. Group formats are not changed to fit the requirements of each activity. Subgroups are left idle.

4. *Energy:* Activities move too slowly. Participants are sedentary. Activities are long or demanding when they need to be short or relaxed. Participants do not find the activity challenging.

5. *Processing:* Participants are confused and/or overwhelmed by the questions posed to them. There is a poor fit between the facilitator's questions and the goals of the activity. Facilitators share their opinions before first hearing the participants' views.

To avoid these pitfalls, follow these steps:

I. Introduce the activity.
   1. Explain your objectives
   2. Sell the benefits
   3. Convey enthusiasm
   4. Connect the activity to previous activities
   5. Share personal feelings and express confidence in participants

II. Help participants to know what they are expected to do.
1. Speak slowly
2. Use visual backup
3. Define important terms
4. Demonstrate the activity

III. Manage the group process.
1. Form groups in a variety of ways
2. Vary the number of people in any activity based upon that exercise's specific requirements
3. Divide participants into teams before give further directions
4. Give instructions separately to groups in a multipart activity
5. Keep people busy
6. Inform the subgroups about time frames

IV. Keep participants involved.
1. Keep the activity moving
2. Challenge the participants
3. Reinforce participants for their involvement in the activity
4. Build physical movement into the activity

V. Get participants to reflect on the activity's implications.
1. Ask relevant questions
2. Carefully structure the first processing experiences
3. Observe how participants are reacting to the group processing
4. Assist a subgroup that is having trouble processing an activity
5. Hold your own reactions until after hearing from participants

DIALOGUE: A METAPHORICAL GAME ABOUT HUMAN INTERACTION

Sivasailam (Thiagi) Thiagarajan

As president of Workshops by Thiagi (4423 East Trailridge Road, Bloomington, IN 47408, 812-332-1478, http://www.thiagi.com), **Sivasailam (Thiagi) Thiagarajan,** *Ph.D. specializes in designing and delivering training for improving human performance. Thiagi has been the president of the International Society for Performance and Instruction (ISPI) and of the North American Simulation and Gaming Association (NASAGA). He is the author of 24 books, 175+ articles, and several hundred games and simulations. Thiagi was a contributor to* **The 1996 McGraw-Hill Team and Organization Development Sourcebook** *and* **The 1996 McGraw-Hill Training and Performance Sourcebook.**

Overview   This game is designed so that participants experience and explore factors that contribute to a positive dialogue between two people. Discussion of the game can focus on the factors that contribute to interpersonal dialogue as well as many other aspects of human interaction, such as issues of competition/collaboration and need for control. The game is suitable for 2 to 200 participants. The ideal number is from 10 to 30.

Suggested Time   20 minutes to 2 hours. The ideal time is about 45 minutes.

Procedure   1. **Brief the participants.** Do not talk about dialogues. Introduce the game as a fun activity.

2. **Demonstrate the procedure.** Ask for a volunteer from the audience to join you in front of the room. Make sure that everyone can hear your conversation. Explain that you and the volunteer are going to take turns supplying one word at a time to construct a meaningful sentence. The object of the game is to come up with the longest possible sentence—and still manage to keep it meaningful.

   Begin by saying a word, any word. Ask the volunteer to add the next word. Take turns to extend the sentence in a playful fashion, one word at a time.

Here is an example:

You: She
Volunteer: wanted
You: desperately
Volunteer: to
You: assassinate
Volunteer: the
You: one
Volunteer: minister
You: who
Volunteer: showed
You: psychotic
Volunteer: masochism

3. **Form partnerships.** Lead a round of applause for the volunteer and ask him or her to return to the group. Ask the participants to pair with a partner.

4. **Conduct the first round.** Ask the participants to repeat the procedure that you and the volunteer demonstrated. Remind them to develop a lengthy, creative, and meaningful sentence. Tell the participants not to write anything down.

5. **Monitor the activity.** Wander among the pairs and listen in on the conversation. Keep moving from one partnership to another, without disturbing anyone.

6. **Conduct the second round.** After about 2 minutes, stop the activity. Tell the participants that they will play another round with a minor variation. Explain that you noticed some players being relegated to the task of merely supplying prepositions, articles, and conjunctions because of the nature of the language. To prevent this from happening, during the next round, each player will supply two words at a time during his or her turn.

7. **Monitor the second round.** Ask the players to begin. As before, wander around and listen in on different conversations, without disturbing anyone.

8. **Conduct the third round.** Stop the second round after a suitable time. Announce that the third round will have two minor changes from the second one: The players have the choice to supply one or two words. Also, one of the players will write down the sentence as it keeps growing.

9. **Monitor the third round.** Ask the partners to begin. Because of the writing requirement, this round will be slower than the previous ones. Give the players sufficient time before stopping this round.

10. **Share the sentences.** Invite partnerships to read their creations. Listen to each sentence (or partial sentence) and lead a round of applause.

11. **Debriefing.** The learning points in this activity will get lost without appropriate debriefing. Here are some of the main learning points you are trying to get across:

✓ The absence of hidden agendas or the need to persuade the other person or the need to impress the other person results in an open-minded process and a delightful result.

✓ Taking turns (instead of one person dominating the conversation) results in positive participation and shared ownership.

✓ Partners who have equal status achieve a smooth dialogue.

✓ Recording the dialogue interferes with its flow but preserves the final product.

✓ Sometimes partners reach a flow state. They are on a roll, often knowing what the other person will say even before the words are said.

✓ The outcomes of a good dialogue delight the participants.

✓ Giving up the urge to control another human being has positive benefits.

Here are some suggested questions for the debriefing session:

✓ Did you feel, at any time, that you were competing with your partner?

✓ Did you feel, at any time, a "loss of control?"

✓ How did the first round (with the partners supplying only one word at a time) compare with the second round (with the partners supplying two words)?

✓ How did the first two rounds (without writing anything down) compare with the third round when you wrote the words?

✓ What if we had more people participating in the construction of the sentence? Instead of two partners, what if we had three participants? Ten participants?

✓ What if we changed partners between one round and the next?

✓ What if one of the partners had a hidden agenda to use certain words in the sentences?

✓ What if the partners were given a topic and asked to construct a sentence related to it?

✓ What if an observer silently listened to the partners while they were constructing the sentence?

✓ What if we recorded the dialogue on audiotape?

✓ Instead of constructing a long sentence, what if we asked the partners to list a set of words associated with each other?

✓ What if the partners were asked to construct a story by taking turns to supply sentences?

Variation

Use groups of 3 to 5 instead of pairs.

CREATING²THE HALF-FULL GLASS: THE POWER OF POSITIVE THINKING

Jeanne Baer

Jeanne Baer *is president of Creative Training Solutions (1649 South 21st Street, Lincoln, NE 68502, 800-410-3178, jbaer@grex.cyberspace.org, http://www.cyberspace.org/~jbaer). The company provides training, facilitation, and program design services. Jeanne teaches at Southeast Community College and is a past president of the Lincoln, Nebraska chapter of the American Society for Training and Development. She is a contributor to* **20 Active Training Programs,** *vol. III (Pfeiffer, in press). Jean was also a contributor to* **The 1996 McGraw-Hill Team and Organization Development Sourcebook** *and* **The 1996 McGraw-Hill Training and Performance Sourcebook.**

Overview   This activity encourages participants to examine their own "explanatory style" in reacting to events, and to replace pessimistic reactions and associations with more positive, optimistic ones. By developing better resilience in times of turbulence, participants can build their self-confidence and adapt more easily to change, benefiting themselves and their organizations.

Suggested Time   1½ to 2 hours.

Materials Needed
- ✓ Form A (What's Your Explanation?)
- ✓ Form B (ABCDE Episodes)
- ✓ Form C (Your Own Alphabet!)
- ✓ Form D (Turbulent Times Checklist)

Procedure
1. Introduce the topic of change by observing that in turbulent times, some people seem less stressed by changes than others. Comment that some people seem to be "born optimists," while others feel pessimistic about changes and uncertainties.

2. Define "optimists" not as people who are "Good-Ship-Lollipop" naive, but rather as those who believe that they're ultimately responsible for their own success. It's not that optimists refuse to see the negative, but they refuse to dwell on it or to give up.

3. Distribute Form A and ask participants to circle their appropriate responses.

4. Explain that the first two situations have to do with "personalization." These scenarios deal with whether you may tend to internalize or externalize credit or blame. Explain that people who blame themselves when they fail or when something goes wrong usually have low self-esteem. People who blame external events don't lose self-esteem when bad events strike. Offer some anecdotes to support this theory.

5. Then explain that the second two situations have to do with how permanent you believe an event's outcome is. Explain that people who give up easily often believe the causes of the bad events that happen to them are permanent—the bad events will persist, and will always be there to affect their lives. They use words like "always" and "never" vs. "sometimes" and "lately."

6. Explain that the last two situations have to do with how pervasive you believe an event's outcome is. People who make widespread explanations for their failures give up on everything, even when a failure strikes in one area. But people who make specific explanations may become helpless in that one part of their lives, yet march strongly on in other parts of their lives.

7. Explain the ABC's of our thinking process when something goes wrong:

   A = Adversity (Something goes wrong, and we react by thinking about it.)

   B = Beliefs (Often so habitual or ingrained that we hardly realize we have them.)

   C = Consequences (Our beliefs lead to what we feel and what we do next.)

8. Explain that before we do something based on pessimistic explanatory habits, we should engage in "D"—Disputation. (Argue with unhealthy beliefs that are causing continuing pessimism and preventing us from reaching our full potential.)

   Explain that there are four important ways to make disputations convincing:

   ✓ Helpfulness—Even if your belief *is* well founded and you're correct, how *helpful* is it to be obsessed with it at the moment?

   ✓ Other causes—What else could have caused this problem you're blaming yourself for?

   ✓ Proof—What material proof do you have that this *is* personal (your fault), permanent (vs. temporary), or pervasive (coloring everything else you'll ever do)?

   ✓ So what?—Even if the negative belief about yourself is correct, is it truly that catastrophic, in the long run? Make a point to "decatastrophize" it.

(It is important that you develop examples or anecdotes to accompany each of the preceding.)

9. Explain to participants that when they take ownership for their own attitudes and maintain positive outlooks, the result will be "E"—Energization. Remind participants that when whey they believe in opportunities, they actually help them appear.

10. Invite participants to consider the two examples on Form B. (If you have time, white out the Disputation and Energization steps. Invite participants to consider individually or in small groups what the possible disputations and energizations might be. You may choose to consider both examples, or focus on the example most appropriate to participants. You may also wish to invite role plays, if you have time.)

11. Once you feel participants understand the steps, invite them to consider an example of their own, using Form C. Ask that they share their examples with a partner; each can check for the other's application of the five steps, and correct or confirm understanding.

12. Close by going quickly over the points on Form D, and adding any personal anecdotes that would be meaningful to the group. (This is a self-explanatory checklist, which can simply be distributed without elaboration if time is short.)

Read the description of the following situations, and vividly imagine this situation happening to you. Even if you haven't experienced it, circle a or b, according to what you honestly think your explanation would be for this event.

1. You invite someone to join you on a team project, and he/she turns you down.
   a. It's me—I'm not very competent in this area.
   b. He/she was already overcommitted to other projects.

2. You get a bonus.
   a. I got lucky; the company had a great year and it can afford to toss a bonus my way.
   b. I deserve it; I've done the right things, and I've done things right.

3. You forget to attend a meeting.
   a. I'm just not good at remembering dates.
   b. I was preoccupied with an urgent project I was working on.

4. You make some great contributions to a brainstorming meeting.
   a. I was especially "up" that day.
   b. I'm a creative person.

5. The data you submitted on a report turns out to be inaccurate.
   a. I gues I'm just sloppy.
   b. This is an isolated incident; I should have proofread it more carefully.

6. Your team members are all upset about organizational changes, and you're able to calm them down and point them in a positive direction.
   a. I had heard about the changes earlier, so I had a chance to think through the issues and prepare for the team meeting.
   b. I'm good in tough situations.

ABCDE Episode in Sales

Adversity: I made my 20th call and I've got just four appointments.

Belief: This is a waste of time. I don't have the energy to succeed. I'm so disorganized.

Consequences: I feel frustrated, tired, depressed, and overwhelmed.

Disputation: Four appointments in an hour isn't bad! It's only 3:00, and I can still do another hour and a half of calling. I can take 10 minutes now to get better organized so I can make more calls this hour than I did in the last hour.

Energization: I feel less overwhelmed and depressed, and I've got more energy, since I'm planning out a course of action.

ABCDE Episode in Management

Adversity: My department is falling behind schedule and my boss is starting to complain about it.

Belief: Why can't these people do what they're supposed to do? I've shown them all they need to know, but why can't I get them to work better? That's why I was hired. Now my boss probably thinks it's all my fault—that I'm incompetent.

Consequences: I feel really mad at my people, and I want to call them all in and chew them out. I also feel bad about myself and nervous about my job. I want to avoid my boss until we get back on schedule.

Disputation: It is true that my department is behind. But I've got several new employees, and it takes time for them to get up to speed. I haven't done anything wrong. I've explained all this to my boss, and she knows it's true. But she's under pressure, too. I'll talk to her again and ask her directly if there's something she thinks I should be doing differently. Meanwhile, I'll keep encouraging the new people and see if I can get more help from the "vets."

Energization: I don't feel like chewing them out now—I feel like I can discuss the situation with them calmly. I'm not nervous about my job because I know I have a good record here. And instead of avoiding my boss, I'll meet with her to give her a progress report and answer any questions she may have.

What are some examples of adversity, beliefs, and consequences in your own life? When you hit that negative self-talk "wall," can you counterpunch with effective disputations and then enjoy the resulting energization? Take time to write an example of your own, based on a past experience or on one that you anticipate will happen in the future:

Adversity:

Beliefs:

Consequences:

Disputation:

Energization:

The following checklist is made up of tips and techniques to help you develop and maintain a more optimistic outlook. Place a check mark beside those that are the most meaningful to you. Then use the space to add specific reminder notes to yourself. Use the list to create your own action plan!

❑ **1.** Ask yourself, Is it *helpful* to have this belief right now?

❑ **2.** Ask yourself, Are there *other* causes for this situation?

❑ **3.** Ask yourself, What is the actual *proof* that this bad situation is permanent, pervasive, or personally my own doing?

❑ **4.** Ask yourself, So what? In the long run, is this *really* important?

❑ **5.** Stop the rumination! Snap a rubber band on your wrist, carry an index card … just say "No!" to circular worrying.

❑ **6.** Jot down what's bothering you, and schedule a time to worry about it. (Then don't bother to keep that "appointment!")

❑ **7.** Visualize doing well. Relax, and picture in great detail the success you deserve and *expect.*

❑ **8.** Refuse to be a victim! Think of yourself as a problem solver, capable of overcoming the barriers that sometimes pop up. Don't waste time and energy being a finger-pointer.

❑ **9.** Team up. Meet with a friend; keep each other on track and hold each other accountable for progress.

❑**10.** Do a kindness every day, to build self-confidence and a positive self-image.

❑**11.** End each day by reminding yourself of three positive things you've done today or three positive qualities you have.

❑**12.** Let it go! Anger and disappointment about the past poisons your present potential.

❑**13.** Sort out what you can and can't control, and then go with change rather than against it. In this world of high-velocity change, surrender serves us better than "fight" or "flight."

❑**14.** Act as if you feel good, as if you're positive and enthusiastic about the future. By acting so you become so.

❑**15.** Start today! What's one positive thing you want to continue doing or start doing?

JUGGLING: LEARNING-HOW-TO-LEARN

Angela Deitch

Angela Deitch, *as president of Angela Deitch Consulting (82 Lochatong Road, West Trenton, NJ 08628, 609-883-6327), works with business leaders to maximize organizational and management effectiveness. Prior to launching her firm, Angela served for eight years as organization and management effectiveness consultant with the state of New Jersey's Human Resource Development Institute. She is an active member of a number of professional organizations and serves on the board of Mid-NJ Chapter American Society for Training and Development; Human Resources Management Association ; Chamber of Commerce of the Greater Princeton Area's Small Business Council Steering Committee and member of Seminars in Leadership Committee; and American Association of University Women.*

Overview
This activity is a short, fun, and active experience that can be used to introduce workshop participants to the notion of *learning how we learn*. The exercise can be expanded or contracted to fit a variety of time frames. In addition, it can be used as a stand-alone exercise, icebreaker, opener for a one- or two-day workshop on learning, or module in another skills workshop.

Suggested Time
1 to 2 hours depending upon the purpose for the exercise and type of processing desired.

Materials Needed
✓ 3 lightweight pieces of fabric such as nylon net, purchased from a fabric store and cut into 18-inch squares, per participant

✓ Form A (Reaction Sheet)

✓ Flip chart and markers

Procedure
1. Introduce the exercise as an introduction to skills training, an icebreaker, or change of pace activity. Don't tell participants they will be exploring their own learning strategies since *you will be observing participants' reactions at each step of the exercise.*

2. Have participants stand with enough space to move their arms freely. Move furniture if necessary.

3. Give each participant three squares of fabric. Explain that they will be learning to juggle, and that you will have them practice each movement after you demonstrate it.

4. First, demonstrate the motion of the arm alone. Raise each arm, one at a time, and pretend you are tossing the fabric into the air. Focus on the imaginary fabric in the air. Have participants practice the motion to get the feel of it.

5. Next, starting with the *right* hand, toss one fabric square into the air above your head. Keep your eye on it, and watch it float down. Reach out and take it in the same hand. Have participants practice. Encourage them to get the feel of the motion, and note how the fabric behaves when it is tossed in the air and floats down. After several tosses with the right hand, demonstrate the same movement with the *left* hand. Toss the fabric square, this time with left hand. Keep your eye on it as it floats down, then reach out and take it in the left hand. Have participants practice several tosses and catches with the left hand.

6. Next, have participants practice with two squares. Toss one square into the air with the *right* hand. As soon as the first square is in the air, toss the second into the air with the *left* hand. Keep your eye on the square in the air. Meanwhile, the first fabric square is floating down. Pick it out of the air with the *left* hand, the hand that has just tossed the second square. Repeat the movements, catching and tossing the fabric square with the *hand opposite* the one that has just tossed it. (One complete series would be: Toss with right hand. Toss with left hand. Catch/re-toss with left hand. Catch/re-toss with right hand.) Have participants practice for several minutes until most of them seem to be able to reproduce the movements.

7. Finally, add the third fabric square. (I usually hold the second and third with my left hand: One is held by my thumb, and the other is held by the small finger.) Begin by tossing the first fabric square into the air with the right hand. Then toss the second into the air with the left hand, releasing the square that is held by the thumb of the left hand. *Immediately,* toss and release the third square which is held with the little finger of the left hand. (This will require some practice, to toss the second and then the third into the air with the left hand—two quick motions—*before the first floats down and must be picked out of the air with the same left hand.*) Once the three fabric squares have been tossed into the air, use one hand and then the other to take a square out of the air and toss it again.

8. Offer encouragement each step of the way. Have participants strive to complete several series of tosses and catches. When a fabric square falls to the floor, start the series over again. Demonstrate how you compete against yourself to successfully complete an increasing number of series. You may decide to end

the exercise when most of the participants can successfully manipulate, i.e., juggle, the fabric squares five to ten times.

9. Ask participants not to discuss their comments with other participants. Distribute Form A and ask participants to indicate their responses.

10. Depending on the amount of available time, you may have participants discuss their responses in small groups *after* they complete Form A. A reporter would then speak for each group.

11. In the processing, ask for possible interpretations of the agree/disagree responses.

12. Have the reporter read the group's statements. Expect a number of responses such as:

"I felt nervous/anxious/frustrated/silly/angry/clumsy, etc."

"My hands began to get sweaty."

"I was afraid of making a fool of myself."

"Everyone else seemed to catch on, but not me."

"I'm not very athletic."

"I thought about when we used to choose sides to play baseball, and no one would choose me."

"My mother/father used to tell me I was a slow learner."

"My second grade teacher said I was dumb."

13. Ask several participants to tell about their experiences, particularly as young children, when someone made fun of their physical or mental ability.

14. Note that some participants may report being eager or excited to learn to juggle: "I enjoy learning new things." A number of the others may nod in agreement, or repeat the thought. Some of these participants may have dismissed their anxiety, and wish to give the politically correct response. If you have carefully observed the participants as they practiced, you may have noticed a number of indications of anxiety: people watching each other, getting frustrated, making negative comments about their ability, questioning the appropriateness of the exercise for their particular group, people who give up or sit down, etc. Share your observations with the group; it's not necessary to attribute a particular behavior to a specific person.

15. Ask participants whether their private conversations (stories) help or hinder their learning? In what way?

16. Ask participants to describe how they learned to ride a bicycle, or swim. What helped them learn? Have them describe the *learning process*. Note on a flip chart terms they associate with learning, such as: time, observation, practice, repetition, improvement, longer, better, etc. Also: recognition, reward, emotion (happy,

proud, etc.). Note, also, that teachers, parents, and relatives, the very people we look up to as children, may be associated with negative feedback. Point out that past experiences impact the way we view the world, change, challenges, new behaviors. These affect our openness to learning, and serve as barriers or diminish our capacity to learn. As we become more aware of the stories that negatively affect our openness to learning, we can become more competent in the way we learn.

17. In the discussion that ensues, relate comments to the following concepts:

Learning how we learn: a process of developing our competence. Frequently our openness to learning is increased or diminished by our own interpretations of the situation, and our personal and historical stories about our ability to learn.

Learning: the ability to repeatedly produce a new action at will. Learning is demonstrated by a change in the body, and takes time and practice. A person who says *she knows* how to swim, *can provide evidence by demonstrating* a particular stroke in the swimming pool.

Competence: how well we perform a skill, based on the assessment of an expert. Someone who is a recognized authority in the performance of the skill can distinguish a number of different levels of proficiency. Use examples to describe different levels of competence. Example: "A young teenager takes out his parents' car and is involved in an accident." "The race car driver manipulated the vehicle around the track at lightning speeds." Ask participants to describe the young teenager's, the race car driver's, and other intermediary levels of driving skill. The purpose of this discussion about levels of competence as it relates to learning is to increase participants' awareness that learning—of all skills—is a *process* that takes time and practice, and that is improved with coaching. (Refer to coaches of professional athletes.) The more adept we are in learning how we learn, the more we can facilitate our learning of functional skills, work-related skills, and the yet undetermined skills of the future workplace.

Please do not discuss the exercise until after you have completed the Reaction Sheet.

Part I. Write a statement that describes your feelings as you participated in the exercise.

_____

_____

Part II. Indicate your agreement/disagreement with the following statements that describe your feelings as you participated in the exercise.

Select:
(1) Strongly Agree ... (2)Agree ... (3) Neither Agree Nor Disagree ... (4) Disagree ... (5) Strongly Disagree

_____

1. Based on this exercise, I feel pretty good about my ability to juggle.   (1) (2) (3) (4) (5)

2. I was apprehensive about succeeding at the exercise.   (1) (2) (3) (4) (5)

3. I found myself checking to see how well other participants were doing the exercise.   (1) (2) (3) (4) (5)

4. There wasn't sufficient time to do the exercise well.   (1) (2) (3) (4) (5)

5. I thought of other incidents when I was judged on my physical ability to perform.   (1) (2) (3) (4) (5)

6. I would like to learn more skills, similar to this one or others that I haven't tried yet, just to experience new learning.   (1) (2) (3) (4) (5)

7. I prefer to stand in the back of the room so I can watch others' performance without being so visible, myself.   (1) (2) (3) (4) (5)

8. I'm uncomfortable being called on to perform skills requiring eye-hand coordination.   (1) (2) (3) (4) (5)

9. It would have been helpful to read the directions before doing the exercise.   (1) (2) (3) (4) (5)

10. By the end of the exercise, I could juggle as well as, or better than, the other participants.   (1) (2) (3) (4) (5)

YOUR PROFESSIONAL ETHICS: RULES OR RESULTS?

Peter Dean

Peter J. Dean, *Ph.D. is an Associate Professor and Department Head of Human Resource Development at the University of Tennessee, Knoxville, TN 37996. He can be reached at 423-974-6272 or pjdean@utk.edu. Peter is editor of the book* **Performance Engineering at Work** *(IBSTPI Publications, 1994) and editor of the* **Performance Improvement Quarterly.** *He was also a contributor to* **The 1996 McGraw-Hill Training and Performance Sourcebook.**

Overview   This activity gives audience members a quick insight into their primary vantage point of perceiving a situation alive with the need for an ethical response. The vantage points *utilitarianism* (results-based) and *formalism* (rules-based) are easily grasped once a story is told and responses elicited from the audience. Discussion could lead into a dialogue about ethical dilemmas being the difference between two rights, and making the best possible decision with the most accurate data available.

Suggested Time   40 minutes.

Materials Needed   ✓ Flip chart

Procedure   1. Tell participants that this story will give them an opportunity to explore an ethical dilemma.

   2. Create your own story using the following factors:

   ✓ Older, wealthy person hires a younger personal secretary to help manage the investments. Worked together 10 years.

   ✓ Celebrating their tenth year together as employer and employee and as personal friends, they decide to go on a cruise together.

   ✓ During the cruise they slip off the boat and land on a desert island. Older person is injured and may die.

   ✓ Older person decides to ask younger person to take care of all investments if necessary, with a special request to liquidate all of it and donate the money to local country club.

✓ Younger person agrees.

✓ Older person dies.

✓ Younger person in shock from exposure and feels sure death will be next.

✓ Younger person saved by a fishing boat.

✓ Younger person has an epiphany—saved for a reason—to help society, etc.

✓ Cashes in all investments but gives all the money to children's hospital, not country club.

3. Ask participants: *Was the younger person ethical?*

The responses usually center around two vantage points. First, the younger person broke a promise and so violated a rule and was wrong to do so. This would be the formalistic argument that calls for standards centered around one's duty to be responsible. The second set of responses usually go along the reasoning that the money will be better spent on the children's hospital and not the country club. The society as a whole is better served, with many recipients. This is the utilitarian argument which centers around the results of the action, mostly irrespective of the means. Both vantage points are valid ethical arguments and we often move from one vantage point to the other as we make decisions.

The group's response varies. Some groups tend to be formalistic and others tend to be utilitarian. To make the best possible decision one needs to be able to see both sides clearly, get as much data as possible, and then decide. One who sees only one side often sees things as black and white, when gray is often the color of reality.

4. Explain the *utilitarian* vantage point in this manner:

The decision to divert the cash brings about an example of a greater good for more people who are in great need. The results are more tangible and obvious. What is lost is the rule to keep our promises, which is the basis of all business transactions. However, we cannot just be utilitarian in our decision making, as people will just do what they want without standards.

5. Explain the *rules-based* vantage point in this manner:

We keep our promises. That is the standard rule. Any deviation is a violation. Yet, some rules are in need of modification sometimes, so we cannot just adopt a rules-based vantage point. We need both vantage points.

6. Ask participants to identify work-related situations they have faced that might be addressed from both vantage points. Consider examples in which a rule, procedure, promise, or argument might be broken because doing so has some benefit (e.g., fudging reports, breaking confidentiality). Discuss the situations from both vantage points.

5
CONSULTATIVE SELLING: THREE ROLE PLAYS TO PRACTICE, PRACTICE, PRACTICE

Bonnie Ferguson

Bonnie Ferguson *(504 Stillhouse Lane, Marlton, NJ, 08053, 609-985-5603) is Director of Human Resources at MIC Re Corporation, a reinsurance company. Previously, she was the director of training and development in the Group Insurance Division at CIGNA. Her work has included classroom instruction, program design, group facilitation, and organizational consulting. Bonnie was a contributor to* **The 1996 McGraw-Hill Training and Performance Sourcebook.**

Overview   Today's sales environment encourages customer-focused consultative selling. The advantages of this approach include increased effectiveness in determining gaps in a customer's needs, *earning* the relationship through relationship building, a sustained competitive advantage through customer rather than product focus, and realistic expectations for both parties.

When explaining a consultative sales approach, it is often helpful to contrast PUSH versus PULL styles of selling. Say "used cars" and the PUSH style comes to mind: a mute buyer and a product-pushing salesperson. The PULL style (consultative) involves finding out what the customer needs and selecting product (or variation of the product) that suits the customer's needs. The customer feels that he or she, *not* the product, is the focus of the transaction.

After a salesperson has completed the Development and Approach elements of a sales process, the time comes for face-to-face contact, or the **Motivating/Consultative** step. Peel this process apart and you find the traditional skills of **questioning** and **listening**. Enhancing these skills in the critical Consultative step of the Sales Process is the subject of the exercises that follow. Following a successful Consultative phase, the salesperson goes on to Close, Implement, and Service the Sale.

Making the transition to consultative selling is hard for those in the habit of mostly talking, not questioning and listening. Three role play exercises are provided here to allow your participants to practice the consultative process.

Suggested Time   60 minutes.

Materials Needed
- ✓ Form A (Observer Guide)
- ✓ Form B (The Case of Prince Printers: Salesperson)
- ✓ Form C (The Case of Prince Printers: Customer)
- ✓ Form D (The Case of Dream Vacations: Salesperson)
- ✓ Form E (The Case of Dream Vacations: Customer)
- ✓ Form F (The Case of Safe 'N' Clean: Salesperson)
- ✓ Form G (The Case of Safe 'N' Clean: Customer)

Procedure

1. Review with participants the major **questioning** skills in the consultative selling process:
   - ✓ Asking questions that get information about the problems of and desired results sought by customers.
   - ✓ Asking open-ended questions that require customers to provide more information than do close-ended questions.
   - ✓ Asking high-yield questions that get past customers' automatic answers and get them to stop and think about their needs and desired options.

2. Review with participants the major **listening** skills in the consultative selling process:
   - ✓ Acknowledging what customers say about their needs.
   - ✓ Responding to questions customers are asking you (be genuine and build rapport).
   - ✓ Checking to be sure you understand what customers are saying.
   - ✓ Summarizing at the end of the conversation to clarify and agree.

3. Divide participants into trios and explain that each person will rotate through each of three roles: *Salesperson, Customer,* and *Observer.* Ask each trio to select roles for the first practice session.

4. Distribute Form A to everyone so that they can review what is being observed. Distribute Form B to the first salesperson in each trio. Distribute Form C to the first customers. Give each salesperson about five minutes to prepare an opening and line of questions for the scenario. During this time, give the observer copies of Forms A and B to review what information was given to the salesperson and customer. Ask the customer to absorb the facts given and think about how he or she can portray the situation as realistically as possible.

5. Conduct the first role play. Allow about ten minutes. Ask both the customer and the observer to give the salesperson feedback on the questioning and listening skills displayed. Suggest that they begin with positive feedback first and then indicate areas of improvement.

6. Repeat this process until all participants have been a salesperson and have received feedback. Distribute the remaining scenarios at the appropriate times.

7. Reconvene the whole group. Debrief the practice session by asking:
   - ✓ How did it go?
   - ✓ Were the skills easy or difficult? Which worked best?
   - ✓ What kind of plans will you make to modify your approach?

OBSERVER GUIDE

Salesperson _____ Observer _____

	Things I Liked	Things I'd Like You to Do Differently
Questioning Skills Asking customer about problems and desired results Open versus closed questions High-yield questions		
Listening Acknowledging customers' needs (verbally) Responding (genuine response, rapport building) Checking for understanding (repeating, paraphrasing) Summarizing (for clarification and agrement)		

THE CASE OF PRINCE PRINTERS: SALESPERSON

You are a sales rep for Prince Printers. Prince made its reputation as a neighborhood print shop for customers who needed copies made, resumes prepared, or print work for small, local businesses. With the advent of desktop publishing, this market is eroding, so Prince has decided to pursue the upscale market—all kinds of business printing including glossy print, brochures, etc. You are expecting to build your niche by attracting medium-size firms as an entrée into the commercial market. Predictably it's been fairly rough going so far. Prince has secured a few key accounts, but they were sold by other reps. You do have a complete sales kit, with samples of a previous job, and you are comfortable that it represents the company's capabilities well.

You have an appointment with the purchasing manager for Videoland, a video distribution sales and rental firm. According to the woman who runs the local Prince Printers (who got you this appointment), Videoland has been a customer of Standard Printing for the last six years. They have in-house capabilities for straightforward requests, but go outside for everything else.

Focus on the customer's needs. What does the customer want to increase, decrease, or maintain? What do you think their concerns will be? What kinds of high-yield questions will you ask?

You are the purchasing manager at the home office of Videoland, a publicly held, medium-sized video distribution sales and rental firm with outlets concentrated across the Northeastern U.S., Illinois, Michigan, and southern Ontario. Videoland employs about 7,000 people in its three divisions, Commercial, Consumer, and Government. Right now, the Consumer division accounts for about 70% of revenues.

Much of the internal print work is done by in-house staff. For example, the corporate Human Resources department produces a newsletter with desktop publishing and you have a copy services unit. Most departments have word processing, simple graphics capability, and laser printers—and they utilize these resources with varying degrees of interest and expertise. The copy services unit in the home office has high quality/high speed copiers, and performs other minor services, such as simple binding, addressing, etc. All other printing requests are sent outside.

It's budgeting time again (no increases) so you're thinking about vendors. You personally prefer to find one vendor to service all these needs. You have traditionally gone to Standard Printing and they have been able to do this fairly well in the past. Standard has continued to grow—your last three service reps have been promoted.

There's a Prince Printers right around the corner from your office, and you've stepped in on occasion. It's run by an acquaintance of yours. She asked if you would meet with one of their national reps regarding your printing needs, so you agreed to this morning's appointment.

What are your needs and interests? Which ones are most important? What concerns do you have?

You've been in the travel business for about four years, all of it at Dream Vacations. It's nice to be able to help people plan an event they look forward to so much. It's amazing how many details are involved, though. And many of the details are out of your control, but people still associate these things with the agency that booked them. You try to steer people away from destinations where the experience might be unpredictable. (Unfortunately, most of these are the reasonably priced options.)

You do have sales targets to meet. Some of your compensation is based on the *Travel Dreams* packaged by your company, which tend to be your higher profit packages. They have some really great Caribbean destinations. You are expected to sell a certain number of these per quarter and you haven't met your target yet.

You also have come up with some really unique options for people who want to try something different: bungee jumping, dude ranches, music tours, and one trip to trace a client's ancestral heritage across Europe. You find those jobs interesting, but they're not the bread and butter.

You had a call from a potential client planning to consult with you at noon. The caller said "I'm looking forward to completely relaxing or going somewhere new and different." Not a whole lot to go on—that doesn't eliminate much—and it's 11:45.

Focus on the customer's needs. What does the customer want to increase, decrease, or maintain? What do you think their concerns will be? What kinds of high-yield questions will you ask?

You've just been through a rough week at work. Boy, do you need a vacation. It's about time you took a good one.

You're not quite sure what you want to do with your time. Sometimes it's nice just to kick back somewhere you can just relax. Other times it's nice to explore new places, so that you get a real change of pace from your life. What you do know is that you don't want to lie on a beach somewhere. It's hard to tell by looking at you, but you turn into a french fry in the sun. You also can't stand any of those tours where you have to get along with a lot of overbearing people.

Sad to say, you don't have as much money to spend as you'd like. Well, maybe if you come up with an intriguing prospect, you'd be willing to splurge a little.

You skimmed the travel section last weekend and picked out a couple of agencies to call. You're on your way out to Dream Vacations on your lunch hour to see what they have to offer.

What are your needs and interests? Which ones are most important? What concerns do you have?

You work for Safe 'N' Clean, a company founded by your father thirty years ago. It provides ancillary services for companies in metropolitan central business districts. You can provide security guards, security systems for the office space, company identification systems, safety monitoring, handyman services such as painting and repairs, and a wide range of janitorial services, including plant care. You've also just gotten into computer security auditing.

You've been very happy with the growth of the company. Right now, the bulk of your staff is fully assigned. You've been pleased at how you've managed to keep overhead down by keeping the staff lean and hiring retirees, who tend to be far more conscientious and less expensive employees.

As the Sales Director for the company, you try to keep your ears open to who's coming and going, who's having security and janitorial staff problems, and who is new to the area. You just heard that Checkcorp is relocating some of its staff to a building they own in the area, but had previously leased out.

Checkcorp will be new to the city. You hope to be the firm that closes this account. After all, Checkcorp is a pretty big company and if you do well, it might help you garner more Checkcorp business in the several cities in which you now have a presence.

What the Facilities Manager said in your brief conversation was "No arrangements had been made yet and there's not a whole lot of money to work with."

Focus on the customer's needs. What does the customer want to increase, decrease, or maintain? What do you think their concerns will be? What kinds of high-yield questions will you ask?

You work for Checkcorp. You just found out that you're going to move to the new location. It was uncertain for a while as to whether this was going to happen and who was going to be retained. They've not only asked you to stay (phew!), but to coordinate the move.

You've been out to see the facility a couple of times. It's reasonably new—about eight years old—but the current tenants' use of the building has subjected it to quite a bit of wear and tear. There is quite a bit to be done. The building is eight floors and you expect to house about 400 people, when the move/expansion is complete.

You have some experience in this type of work since you've managed facilities before, but previously, you've taken over fairly smoothly running facilities. This is almost starting from scratch. You've brainstormed a bit and your "to do" list is already two pages long. You need to arrange to improve the appearance of the building and all systems that need to be installed: phones, computer workstations, security, etc. You've got to manage all of this on a pretty tight budget and you want to make sure you do a really good job.

You've worked with outside services before, and you have a real concern about the security staff they provide. Many of them look as though they're asleep on the job, or could be knocked over by your grandmother. It's not enough to have guards there; your view is that either you have effective, consistent security or don't bother. Then there are the arrangements for employee access. You'd like a state-of-the-art system with a minimum of hassle. Unfortunately, your budget may not support that. Your most pressing need, though, is to begin the improvement work. It should have started yesterday. As a matter of fact, your desk is currently littered with paint chip samples.

You got a call from a company called Safe 'N' Clean about the facilities management services they provide. They are eager to talk to you. You have agreed to meet with their Sales Director.

What are your needs and interests? Which ones are most important? What concerns do you have?

GIVING AND RECEIVING FEEDBACK: A LEARNING EXERCISE

Francesco Sofo

Francesco Sofo, *Ph.D. is an academic and consultant in Adult Education/Human Resource Development at the University of Canberra (P.O. Box 1 Belconnen, ACT 2616, Australia, 616-2015123, franks@education.canberra.edu.au). Formerly chair of the HRD/Adult Education Program and Founding Director of the Center for HRD Studies, he is currently senior lecturer and convenor of the Masters in Community Education (HRD) Program. He is the author of* **Critical Reflection Strategies Using Teams** *(1995) and lead author of* **The Critical Reflection Inventory (CRI) Self-Rating Scales Manual** *(1996).*

Overview This activity is a multigroup-based strategy to learn about five principles of giving and receiving effective feedback. Instead of engaging in an activity and then moving on to something else, participants are asked to discuss in detail from several perspectives two principles of giving and receiving feedback and then share those outcomes in a group before reporting the findings to the whole group. By focusing in detail on feedback and then expressing this in concrete form to share with the whole group, the participants learn about a set of principles of giving and receiving feedback.

Suggested Time 90 minutes.

Materials Needed ✓ Form A (General Functions and Principles of Feedback)

✓ Form B (Five Principles for Giving and Receiving Effective Feedback)

✓ Form C (Five Roles for Discussing Feedback)

✓ Flip chart and markers

Procedure 1. Inform participants that this exercise will give them the opportunity to learn about a set of principles for giving and receiving effective feedback.

2. Distribute Form A and ask participants to read it to themselves. Conduct a brief discussion on the general functions and principles of effective feedback.

3. Divide the whole group into five Home Teams of five members or conduct the exercise with one or more intact teams.

4. Distribute a copy of Form B to each home team member. Each team member is to select one of the five principles for giving and receiving effective feedback from Form B. Ensure that each of the five principles is selected only once.

5. Ask all participants who chose the same principle to form an Expert Team to discuss that principle. There will be five Expert Teams as there are five principles on Form B. (You may call them Expert Teams 1, 2, 3, 4, and 5.) If there are fewer participants than required, then select fewer than five principles.

6. Distribute a copy of Form C to each member of the Expert Team. Allow members to adopt one of the roles listed on Form C. They should discuss the feedback principle with this role in mind.

7. Instruct the Expert Teams to discuss the principle they selected from Form B. Inform them that they have 10 minutes to ensure that the team members share all the knowledge they have and their understanding of the principle and to relate their own experiences about it. As far as possible they should adhere to the role function prescribed for them during the discussion.

8. Ask everyone to go back to their Home Teams to contribute their findings from the Expert Teams. (Time allocated for this is 15 minutes.)

9. Invite each Home Team to make a summary on flip chart paper and report it to the entire group.

[If time permits use the following additional steps.]

10. Using the principles just learned, ask all group members to form pairs and to give each other feedback on this exercise.

11. Elicit comments from members of the whole group on how they felt they were able to apply the feedback skills.

REFERENCES

Sofo, Francesco. (1995) *Critical Reflection Strategies Using Teams.* F & M Sofo Educational Assistance. 55 Vagabond Cr. McKELLAR, 2617 ACT, Australia. ISBN 0-646248251.

Sofo, Francesco, and Kendall, Lawrence. (1996) *The Critical Reflection Inventory (CRI) Self-Rating Scales: Forms A, B & C Manual.* F & M Sofo Educational Assistance. 55 Vagabond Cr. McKELLAR, 2617 ACT, Australia. ISBN 0-646291793.

GENERAL FUNCTIONS AND PRINCIPLES OF FEEDBACK

As well as verbal messages, feedback consists of nonverbal messages including silences. Feedback is information that is given to the speaker concerning the listener's reactions to the message. Once people's attention is obtained, all responses and reactions are regarded as feedback. Feedback begins from the moment feed forward (the introduction) is initiated. Feedback has a number of functions in social interaction. Feedback:

✓ provides information about different people's reactions;

✓ acts as a group memory by recalling events;

✓ maintains equilibrium within the relationship(s);

✓ encourages people to appreciate complexity and difference;

✓ stimulates people to gain insights;

✓ achieves self-knowledge and identity of individuals and groups;

✓ assists in knowledge, skills, and attitudes acquisition;

✓ creates possibility for improvement at individual, group, and system levels.

Some general principles for giving feedback are useful when engaging in a social interaction. A general first principle for giving feedback is to demonstrate genuine respect to all members of the group. Respect is demonstrated by:

✓ giving recognition to strengths;

✓ being open and impartial to possible outcomes;

✓ offering different explanations for problems;

✓ asking the person(s) being observed how they think they used their skills;

✓ execution of the specific role by each participant.

This type of feedback is designed to encourage inquiry and curiosity through observation and description. Feedback is most useful when it involves formulating and testing hypotheses. This requires adoption of an open-minded attitude and maintenance of a stance of neutrality.

Giving information or feedback can be used as a way of giving help. It can be a learning mechanism for the person who wants insights into how well their behavior matches their intentions as perceived by the participants or audience. Feedback can be a means of establishing one's identity for answering, *Who am I?* The famous sociologist Charles Cooley said that we come to know who we are by the reflection others give us of ourselves. The following are five principles of giving and receiving effective information (feedback).

PRINCIPLE 1

GIVING FEEDBACK

Feedback describes behavior rather than evaluates behavior.
Describing one's own reactions to another's behavior leaves the other free to use the feedback or not use it, as they see fit. Avoiding evaluative language reduces the need for the individual to react defensively (learning is difficult when one is defensive).

Here is an example:

Your head nodded a lot and I noticed you yawning six or seven times during the discussion (behavior); **not,** *You looked bored and disinterested* (motive).

RECEIVING FEEDBACK

Encourage feedback by asking questions that indicate you want feedback.
Obtaining information about yourself from others can help you know yourself better and enable you to interact more effectively in groups. Your reactions to feedback should encourage others to provide it freely. Ask:

✓ *Are there other benefits people think may result from this communication exchange?*

✓ *What did you notice about my performance/behavior?*

✓ *How did I come across just then?*

GIVING FEEDBACK

Feedback describes specific behaviors.
In giving feedback try to avoid making general and categorical statements about behavior. Telling a person they were "domineering" gives a categorical interpretation of their behavior and may not be very useful to that person. A more useful statement would be:

Just now when we were deciding the issue, I felt that you did not listen to what others said and that you were expecting me either to accept your point of view or face attack from you.

RECEIVING FEEDBACK

Ask about the specifics of your own words and behavior.
If people say you were "okay" or "good" or use other evaluative terms such as "awful" or "enjoyable," you will need to ask them about specific behaviors or words you used to give them that reaction. Ask:

What sort of things did I do and say that made you feel it was okay?

PRINCIPLE 3
GIVING FEEDBACK

Effective feedback expresses consideration toward the receiver.
Feedback can be destructive when it serves only your own needs as giver and fails to consider the needs of the person on the receiving end. During the social interaction endeavor to notice the purposes and motivations of the speakers. Instead of assuming what they were endeavoring to achieve ask them to express what their needs and motivation were during the interaction. Then you can more accurately frame your feedback with their orientations and perspectives in mind.

RECEIVING FEEDBACK

Ask probing and clarifying questions.
Make sure you understand comments others make about your behavior. You can do this by asking them probing questions such as questions of clarification and qualification. Ask:

Can you give me an example of that?

What assumptions did you identify in what I said?

Were there times I did not engage in that behavior?

GIVING FEEDBACK

Feedback should be tentative and focus on behavior that the receiver can modify.

Try to develop a sense of what is within the power of people to change within themselves. For example, personality characteristics are not points of focus that people generally would want to address or change about themselves. Frustration is only increased when people are reminded of some shortcoming over which they have no control.

RECEIVING FEEDBACK

Avoid reacting and becoming defensive to feedback you receive.

You should withhold your own judgments, reasons, or explanations when feedback is provided by accepting others' responses to you without justifying your actions or words. If you try to justify your actions others may think that you are defensive and they may then be reluctant to give you further feedback or to clarify points they made.

PRINCIPLE 5

GIVING FEEDBACK

Once expressed, ownership of the speaker's utterances may be assumed by the listener as well.

The speaker should express thoughts and feelings about the other person's behavior. Everyone needs to assume responsibility for telling each other the impact of behaviors on them. Frame your feedback in terms of your own feelings and thoughts rather than the other person's assumed feelings. Example:

I felt frustrated when I heard the conversation return to the same issue three times.

RECEIVING FEEDBACK

Use this sequence of action after you receive feedback:

a. Take ownership of the feedback and reflect on it.

b. Decide if and how you can grow from the feedback.

c. Say "Thank You" to the person giving the feedback.

FIVE ROLES FOR DISCUSSING FEEDBACK FORM C

Role 1: Critic

Apart from contributing your own ideas about the principle of giving and receiving feedback you should try to ask critical thinking questions both of your own assumptions and of the ideas expressed by others in the group. (Play the devil's advocate.) Use the following types of questions to help you be a critic in the discussion:

What are you assuming when you say that?

What is likely to happen if everybody adopted that view or procedure?

How is your idea similar to the ideas already expressed?

What are your reasons for saying that?

How can we judge the value of that idea?

Role 2: Image Maker and Scribe

Apart from contributing your own ideas about the principle of giving and receiving feedback you should endeavor to keep a record of the discussion in words and picture/diagram format. As well as scribe, your role is to suggest metaphors or images for the ideas that best symbolize the thinking of the group. For example, if people express an idea that a feedback principle is not very useful you may want to suggest an image for this idea such as "no through road," that is, a "dead end," or a "rubbish bin for waste."

Listen to people's language as you may find people use figurative expressions and your role may be to simply highlight the images enunciated for all the group to note. You may suggest that some of the images are worth exploring in order to help everyone clarify the meaning.

Role 3: Ideas Threader

Apart from contributing your own ideas about the principle of giving and receiving feedback your role is to encourage people to link their own contributions to the discussion already expressed. Encourage the group to build a coherent and unified set of explanations clearly showing the links among all the contributions. Help to clarify and consolidate the ideas.

Ask people how their ideas are similar to or different from other ideas already shared. Your role is to make overt the thread that ties together all the ideas expressed. Ask the group to help you identify the nature of such a thread.

Role 4: Critical Reviewer

Apart from contributing your own ideas about the principle of giving and receiving feedback your role is to encourage people to critically review their contributions. You may appeal to particular individuals in the group or to the group generally and ask them if new information presented in the discussion has made any difference to their initial ideas.

Just before the discussion ends, ask people how their ideas have changed as a result of the discussion. Then ask them if they are happy to accept any conclusions the group has arrived at; for example, would they use the ideas themselves?

Role 5: Facilitator and Time Keeper

Apart from contributing your own ideas about the principle of giving and receiving feedback your role is to encourage all people in your group to contribute equitably. You may do this by noticing which group members tend to be reticent and inviting them to express their view of what has already been said and any views of their own on the topic. About two minutes before time is to expire for the discussion you should inform the group that it may be a good idea to summarize their discussion. The critical reviewer (role 4) may wish to ask the group a question to consider.

In short, your role is to ensure that the discussion remains focused, that all contribute equitably, and that people are aware of the need to achieve the group goal within the given time.

BUILDING ACROSS DIFFERENCES: A CULTURAL DIVERSITY ACTIVITY

Robert Kaeser and Marie Amey-Taylor

Robert Kaeser, *Ph.D. is an independent trainer and consultant (1919 Chestnut Street, Suite 1918, Philadelphia, PA 19103, 215-568-1338). Bob has designed and presented workshops on a variety of topics, including sexual harassment prevention, cultural diversity, and team building.* **Marie Amey-Taylor,** *Ed.D. is an Assistant Director of Human Resources Development, Personnel Department, Temple University (1601 N. Broad Street, Philadelphia, PA 19122, 215-204-1673), and President of Kaleidoscope, a training firm (8345 Mansfield Avenue, Philadelphia, PA 19150, 215-248-0221). Marie designs and conducts training programs and specializes in diversity training and team building.*

Overview   This activity can be used with teams in a cultural diversity workshop setting. It is highly interactive, and can be used to make a variety of learning points, including: the level playing field; what it feels like to be different from others; how groups tend to deal with those who are different; Workforce 2000 demographics; the relationship of creativity, diversity, job satisfaction, and task completion; the difference between task and process; information about stereotyping, prejudice and discrimination, and the role of supervisors in managing diverse teams.

Suggested Time   Approximately 1 hour.

Materials Needed
- ✓ Several packs of colored index cards
- ✓ Markers
- ✓ Role cards
- ✓ Flip chart
- ✓ Chairs and tables

Procedure   1. Write the following instructions on index cards to be used as role cards. A complete set will be needed for each team.

Card One:

From now on, you no longer speak or understand English.

Card Two:

From now on, you can no longer use your hands.

Card Three:

From now on, you must turn your chair around, and can no longer see your team.

Card Four:

From now on, you must add "ing" after each word that you say.

2. Tell the group that they are about to complete a group task.

3. This activity works best in a group of six to eight members. If there are more than eight participants, divide them into subgroups.

4. Tell the team(s) that their first task is to select a *process observer*, giving no other instruction than that they should choose a "responsible" person.

5. Ask the process observer(s) to come to the front of the room for instructions. At the same time, inform the team(s) that they will be building a three-dimensional model of (trainer's choice): an office of the future, a monument representing the diversity of the team or the organization they are from, an off-site retreat, a vacation home, an ideal work place, or any other construction you might select.

6. Give the process observer(s) the four "role cards" and tell them they must distribute them to team members some time early on in the activity. It is up to them to decide when and to whom. Once they have given a card to someone, that person must follow the instruction on the card for the rest of the activity. Privately, tell the process observer(s) that they will be responsible for observing the team, and give them some feedback about what happens to the group dynamics when certain members become "different." Suggest that they observe such things as who talks and who doesn't, how decisions are made, what roles various members play, and so forth. Remind them that they are not members of the team and that they cannot participate in the activity. Return them to their teams.

7. Give the team(s) their instructions. Tell them that they will have 15 minutes to build a three-dimensional model of whatever has been chosen, select a location, and name their creation. However, the only materials they will have to complete the task are some index cards and a marker.

8. After 15 minutes, call time. Tell the role card recipients that they no longer have to abide by their restrictions. Give team members an opportunity to talk among themselves about their reactions to

the activity. (If there is more than one team, have the entire group make a site visit to each of the models and have a spokesperson from each team describe the model's unique features.)

9. Have everyone return to their team tables. Then ask the process observers to give their reports and to tell why they chose to give role cards to particular members. Ask them to discuss these questions with the team:

   ✓ How did you decide to distribute the role cards?

   ✓ What were your goals?

   ✓ What patterns emerged?

   ✓ How does the role of the process observer compare to the role of a supervisor of a diverse team?

   ✓ How did the team make decisions? How did the team deal with the role card people?

10. Ask those who held role cards how they experienced not being able to speak or understand English, not being able to use their hands, not being able to see the model, and having to say "ing" after every word.

    Some typical processing questions include:

    ✓ How did it feel to be different?

    ✓ How did the others react to and treat you?

    ✓ Were you able to make adjustments, and did the team make "reasonable accommodations" to ensure inclusion of all its members?

    ✓ How were you valued or discounted?

11. Ask the group for any final thoughts about the activity.

DEVELOPING CAREER RESILIENCE: EXPLORATIONS IN CAREER SELF-MANAGEMENT

Leigh Mundhenk

Leigh G. Mundhenk, *Ph.D. is a consultant and founder of WorkConcepts (15 Belmont St., Portland, ME 04101, 207/776-3863). She consults with individuals and organizations on career management and development issues. She is particularly interested in the impact of organizational transition on career development and is conducting research in this area as part of her studies at Temple University, where she is a doctoral candidate in Psychoeducational Processes. Leigh is an assistant editor of and contributor to* **20 Active Training Programs,** *vol. III (Pfeiffer, in press). She was also a contributor to* **The 1996 McGraw-Hill Training and Performance Sourcebook.**

Overview   This activity is designed to introduce participants to the concept of career self-management. Many organizations have traditionally taken responsibility for the career paths of their employees. Today, as organizational culture becomes more empowering and less paternalistic, employees will find that assessing their own strengths and developing their own developmental plans will be key to maintaining the career resilience needed to stay employable in the next century.

Suggested Time   60 minutes.

Materials Needed   ✓ Form A (Career Self-Management Action Plan)
✓ Flip chart and markers

Procedure   1. Tell participants that this exercise is designed to help them understand how changes taking place in the workplace are affecting how we manage careers.

2. State that in the past organizations have traditionally had an implied contract with their employees that provided lifelong employment in exchange for loyalty and hard work. Add that this has led to organizations adopting a paternalistic role in managing the careers of their employees. Add that today organizations are

moving toward an implied contract based on productivity, where work is situational and employees are empowered to make their own decisions to get results. State that although the organization should develop a supportive role by providing resources and encouragement, ownership for career management in this new relationship rests with the employee.

3. Form groups of three. Pose the following question to the trios and ask them to discuss it for 5 minutes:

"How has your organization changed its implied contract with its employees in the past two years and what evidence have you seen of this?"

After 5 minutes are up, rotate the trios by asking each group to assign members the number 0, 1, or 2. Ask 1's to rotate to the next group clockwise and have 2's rotate to the second group clockwise. Have 0's remain where they are. Each group should have all new members. Pose the second question:

"How do you feel about the new implied contract that places responsibility on employees for their productivity and management of their own career development?"

After 5 minutes rotate the groups again using the same method and pose the following question:

"What steps have you made or would you make to better prepare yourself to enhance your employability for the new implied contract?"

4. Process the discussion by asking volunteers for some of their answers to the last question. Write them on a flip chart and mention additional suggestions such as:

✓ Conduct a thorough self-assessment of skills, knowledge, abilities, values, and temperament. Set aside a personal review day twice a year to update your profile.

✓ Define areas of potential career interest to you that meet organizational needs of the future.

✓ Engage in a lifelong learning program to enhance and promote employability. This can be done by taking courses, earning a degree, reading, etc.

✓ Engage in ongoing networking both in and outside the organization.

✓ Learn and use excellent work and job search skills such as writing resumes and letters and interviewing.

5. Distribute Form A and state that it's helpful to have an action plan to get started. Referring to the flip chart, remind participants that you have discussed several things they can do to start the process.

6. Ask participants to take 5 minutes to fill out Form A.

7. Form seat partners and ask pairs to discuss their plans, asking partners to comment and provide support and encouragement.

8. Close by saying that it is important to develop a new mindset. Even though there is no real job security, employability comes from taking ownership for the management of your career and doing your own steering. Add that it is very empowering and liberating to make one's own career choices. End by saying that the key to real career fulfillment is in identifying the type of work that makes you feel passion; that when you feel passion for your work, your work becomes your avocation.

CAREER SELF-MANAGEMENT ACTION PLAN

1. What are two skills you really enjoy using and feel competent using?

2. What are two values you feel are important in choosing your work?

3. What special knowledge do you have that you like to use in your work?

4. What special abilities do you have that you would like to use more in your work?

5. How does your temperament affect the type of work you like to do?

6. When you think about your ideal work or job, what is it you would like to do?

7. What is preventing you from doing it?

8. What would you have to do in order to be able to do your ideal work or job?

9. How willing are you to make that investment?

10. When are you willing to start?

11. What will you do first?

12. I have made a contract with myself to start my career self-management program on:

PLAIN SPEAKING: LEARNING HOW TO MAKE YOUR POINT

9

Richard Whelan and Robert Merritt

Richard Whelan *is director of Associated Consultants for Training &
Education (P.O. Box 5312, Deptford, NJ 08096, 609-227-4273). He designs,
develops, and delivers training programs pertaining to human resource and
mental health issues for organizations in both the public and private sectors.*
Robert Merritt, *Ph.D. is a senior consultant with Associated Consultants for
Training & Education. He is an applied social psychologist specializing in
organization development and management training, working in both the private and public sectors.*

Overview
This "one-way communication" activity is designed to help participants
learn about the many road blocks inherent in the communication
process. Through a simple and entertaining exercise in "giving directions," participants will experience various interferences to being able
to effectively give and receive messages.

Suggested Time
45 minutes.

Materials Needed
✓ Easel
✓ Flip chart pad
✓ Markers
✓ Forms A, B, C, D

Procedure
1. Ask who in the group see themselves as effective communicators.
   Choose two of the participants who have raised their hands. Of
   these two, ask which one likes to talk. This is the person who will
   be the "speaker" and the other will be the "listener."

2. The listener will be given a marker and asked to go to the easel that
   is in the front of the room. The listener will stand at the easel, back
   to the rest of the group.

3. The speaker will be instructed to take the templates (Forms A, B,
   C, D) and stand in the center of the room, back to the listener so
   that what is drawn will not be seen by the speaker. (The remaining

participants can sit or stand anywhere they choose, as long as they are facing the listener.)

4. Tell the speaker to describe what is drawn on one or more of the templates to the listener so that it can be drawn on the flip chart paper. **Privately,** give the speaker the following instructions:

   ✓ In describing the figure to be drawn, if there is a geometric figure on it, like a triangle or square, it cannot be called a triangle or square. Another description, such as a half-diamond or box, must be used. A circle could be described as "a 360° line that ends at its starting point." (We had one experience in which this activity was done with a group of professional football players and one, in describing a triangle said, "Imagine the top of a goal post where the two end poles fell in to each other.")

   ✓ The speaker cannot look at what is being drawn or ask any questions about what or how the listener is doing; just proceed until the speaker feels all four figures (or whichever of the four have been chosen) have been described.

   ✓ The speaker may show the templates to the remainder of the participants before describing them to the listener. (You might also decide to provide copies for the remainder of the participants.)

   Tell the listener not to ask any questions or say anything until the exercise is completed.

5. The other participants in the room may react in any manner they choose as long as they are not giving help or suggestions to the listener.

6. At the conclusion of the drawing(s), the speaker looks at the completed drawing(s) and shows the listener what they were supposed to look like.

7. The facilitator can ask the following questions of the listener and the speaker as part of the processing of the activity and their learning from it:

   ✓ How did you do in your role?

   ✓ How did you feel while you were in your role?

   ✓ How successful were you?

   ✓ What was difficult about the activity?

   ✓ What would have made the task easier?

8. After the speaker and listener have had a chance to respond to the questions, solicit audience reaction to the process, obtaining their observations and learning.

9. Ask all the participants these questions:

   ✓ What helps you to be clearer in your communication with others?

   ✓ What helps you to listen accurately and retain what has been said to you?

Variation

A modification in the design can be used, such as:

- ✓ For the first template, follow the instructions as described above.
- ✓ For the second, allow the speaker to ask questions while still facing away from the listener.
- ✓ For the third, allow only the listener to ask questions while facing the easel.
- ✓ For the fourth template, allow the speaker to actually view what is being drawn as a way of modifying any future instructions, without making changes to previous instructions or trying to correct any "mistakes" the listener may have made in drawing.

As part of the processing questions, ask what differences, if any, these changes had on the successful completion of the task.

As part of this variation, questions can also be asked after each one of the drawings, such as:

- ✓ How was this different from the previous method?
- ✓ What situations in real life mimic this type of communication?
- ✓ How can you compensate for this type of limitation?

FIGURE 1

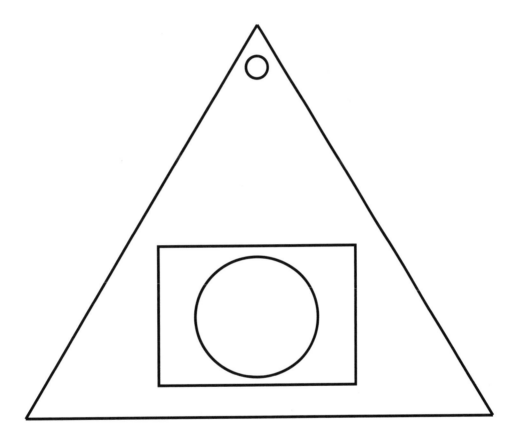

FIGURE 2

FORM B

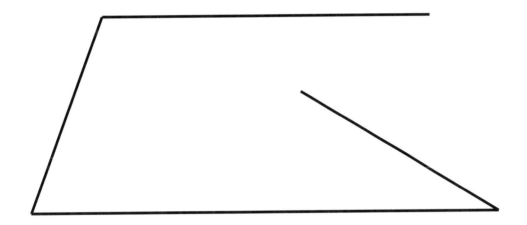

FIGURE 3

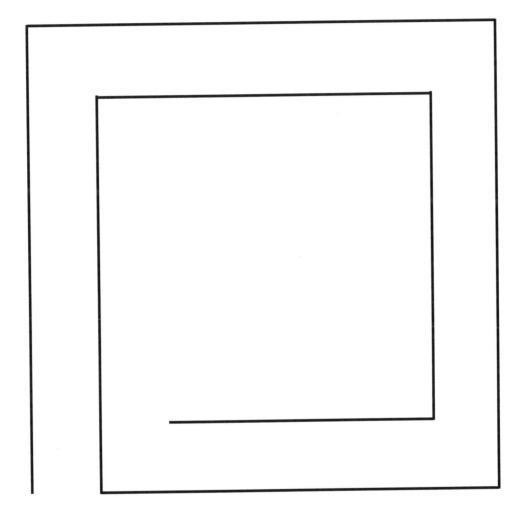

FIGURE 4

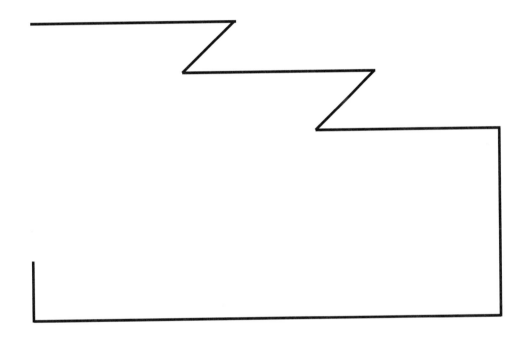

IT'S WHO YOU KNOW: A SIMULATION TO INTEGRATE PEOPLE WITH DISABILITIES

Mary Moynihan

Mary Moynihan *is president of Wesmar Associates (7 Pembroke Road, Lewes, DE 19958, 302-644-1586, wesmar@Prodigy.com), a consulting firm that specializes in training related to disability issues. She is also a trainer for The Accreditation Council (Towson, MD), and the former Training Director at The University Affiliated Program of New Jersey, University of Medicine & Dentistry of NJ. Mary has provided training on a national level for a variety of organizations.*

Overview

People with disabilities are becoming more visible, in communities, at school, and in the workplace. Those who have had little contact with individuals with disabilities are often uncomfortable when faced with a situation in which they must interact with a person who has a disability. In reality, everyone has a deep reservoir of personal resources that can be used to assist someone with a disability to become an active citizen, student, or worker.

This training simulation is designed to provide those who are unfamiliar with people with disabilities with an opportunity to experience their own ability to use their personal and community resources to assist those with disabilities to become contributing members of a community, an organization, or a workplace.

Suggested Time

45 to 60 minutes.

Materials Needed

✓ Index cards, one for each participant

✓ Flip chart paper and markers

Procedure

1. Distribute one index card to each person. Ask participants if any of them have business cards. Have a few participants tell the group what kind of information they have on their business cards. Ask them to pass them around, so that others can see what they look like.

79

2. Prompt participants to discuss how they use a business card, e.g., to give someone their address or phone number, to remind someone to send them something, to let someone know who they are or where they work.

3. Tell participants that they are now each going to design their own "personal resource card." It should include their name, home address, any interests they have, and their community connections. Give examples such as what church they attend, where they like to shop, where they work, community groups they belong to, etc. Allow about 10 to 15 minutes.

4. Invite participants to move around the room and network with each other. Tell them to talk with as many people as possible and instruct them to make a brief note on the back of their card about each person they talk with. If the participants are already familiar to each other, tell them to use this time to learn something new about each other.

5. Reassemble the group and begin a discussion about the variety of interests and resources that are found in every community or work environment. Elicit some of the information that they discovered about each other.

6. Ask the participants if they are familiar with the concept of a welcome wagon. Have a participant explain the concept to the group. Fill in additional details, if necessary, by indicating that there is a practice in some communities in which newcomers are presented with a welcome package of community orientation materials.

7. Divide the group into three small groups. Tell them that each small group is a community welcome wagon committee. Assign each small group a different new community member to welcome.

   ✓ **Group 1** will design a package for a new family with a child who is younger than thirteen and has a disability.

   ✓ **Group 2** will design a package for a new community member who is a young adult and has a disability.

   ✓ **Group 3** will design a package for a new community member over 60 years old who has a disability.

8. Instruct each group to design a welcome package for their assigned new community member.

9. Tell them to use the information they learned from networking and to talk with members of other small groups for additional information. What community groups could they connect this family or person with? Who do they know who could help this person to get involved?

10. Instruct them to use the flip chart paper to record their ideas. Encourage them to be creative. Give them 20 minutes to complete this task.

11. Ask each group to describe their new community member, to present their welcome package, and to describe the process they used to design it.

12. Facilitate a short discussion including the following points:

    ✓ All of us have resources to offer to people with disabilities.

    ✓ All people want to belong and to give, including people with disabilities.

    ✓ Assisting one person is often more effective than trying to work with a group or organization.

THREE LEARNING THEORIES: A PICTURE IS WORTH A THOUSAND WORDS

Brenda Gardner and Sharon Korth

Brenda S. Gardner, *Ph.D. is Assistant Professor and Director of the Executive HRD Graduate Program at Xavier University (3800 Victory Parkway, Cincinnati, OH 45207-6521, 513-745-4287, gardner@xavier.xu.edu). She is on the board of the Academy of HRD and has extensive experience in training and organization development in public and private organizations.* **Sharon J. Korth,** *Ed.D. is Assistant Professor of HRD at Xavier University (513-745-4276, korth@xavier.xu.edu). She has chapters in* **In Action: Conducting Needs Assessment,** *edited by Jack Phillips and Elwood Holton, Alexandria, VA: ASTD, 1995, and in* **ASTD Toolkit: More Needs Assessment Instruments,** *edited by John Wilcox, Alexandria, VA: ASTD, 1994. Sharon and Brenda were contributors to* **The 1996 McGraw-Hill Team and Organization Sourcebook.**

Overview This design provides participants with an understanding of three general learning theories and an appreciation of how these theories relate to training and learning situations in the workplace. Through various activities, participants will be able to describe the different theories and explain how they apply to their role as trainer, supervisor, manager, or job coach. This design can be used as a module in larger training programs that focus on training the trainer, classroom teaching techniques, or on-the-job training methods.

Suggested Time 90 minutes.

Materials Needed
- ✓ Stimulus picture (pink elephant)
- ✓ Treat (candy)
- ✓ Complex picture
- ✓ Paper
- ✓ Colored pens or markers

Procedure   1. Tell participants that this exercise will give them an overview of three general learning orientations and their application in adult learning situations. These activities will help them understand their personal beliefs about how people learn and help them explore when different approaches may be effective. Tell them that these three orientations are:

Behaviorism, Cognitivism, and Social Learning

2. Display an unusual stimulus picture such as a pink elephant and tell the participants that you are going to teach them something. Explain that whenever they see this picture, they are to perform the following task: pat their knees with their hands twice, clap twice, click their fingers on their right hand, click their fingers on their left hand, and then say "green pig" in unison.

Demonstrate this task, let them practice, and then display the picture and have them respond. Watch the group carefully and reward those who perform accurately with a small piece of candy. Tell the others that they need more practice, review the steps, provide feedback on what was not done properly, and allow time for practice. Display the stimulus picture again and watch for the correct execution of the skills. End the activity by giving each person a piece of candy.

Lead a discussion about how this activity relates to *behaviorism.* In the behavioral model, the learner is asked to perform step-by-step actions and is given feedback and reinforcement about his or her performance. Ask participants to name some well-known behaviorists, describe the behaviorist view of the learning process, and describe evidence of the behaviorist learning theory in adult learning. If not mentioned by the participants, point out that behavioral learning objectives, competency-based education, and skill development and training have a behaviorist foundation.

3. Select an object in the back of the room, such as a door or a clock. Tell the participants that you are now going to discuss *cognitivism* and would like them to look at the object. Point to the object and start walking to the back of the room toward the object. When all participants are looking at the object, tell them that they have just experienced the first step in the cognitive (or information processing) model, *attention.*

Return to the front of the room and display a complex picture so that everyone can see it. Ask participants to study the picture. After about 30 seconds, ask them two or three obscure questions about details on the picture, such as, "What was the color of the second stripe on the curtain?" Don't give them the correct answers or show the picture while you are testing them. Tell them that you will give them another chance and display the picture for another 30 seconds. Then ask different obscure questions about the picture, following with a discussion about the second step in the cognitive model, *selective perception*.

Tell participants that you are going to state some numbers and you want them to remember them without writing anything down. Slowly read off the numbers: 21742846789036. Check to see how successful they are in remembering them. Then tell them that these numbers are a phone number and a house number and repeat them in clusters: phone number 217-428-4678, house number 9036. See how successful they are in remembering them. Discuss the third cognitive step, *coding*.

Lead a discussion about the fourth step, *retrieval*, by asking participants for examples of times when they had difficulty recalling something, such as a test question whose answer was on the bottom corner of page 50 next to the coffee stain.

Ask participants if they would study the same way for a multiple choice test and an essay exam. Explain that the type of response required affects how people learn, which is evidence of the final cognitive step, *response generation*.

Wrap up the cognitivist discussion by explaining that cognitivists are interested in the development of internal mental processes. The learner is asked to perform tasks that lead to discovery and insight. Point out that cognitivism is evident in adult learning in the areas of reflective learning and problem solving.

4. Ask participants to make a list of people who have served as role models in their lives. Be sure that they include parents! With a partner, have them discuss what they learned from these people and how that transpired. Ask a few of the participants to give examples to the group.

Explain that *social learning theory* is manifested in adult education in the form of modeling, coaching, and mentoring. Often, we learn things from others by noticing what they do rather than what they say. Usually, the process seems intangible. The learning we obtain from other models is not as systematic as the learning we get from planned instruction, but it can, at times, be more powerful.

5. Tell the participants that you are going to summarize the discussion of the three orientations to learning by having them draw a picture that illustrates a learning theory. Have the participants number off 1 to 3 and assign the 1's to draw behaviorism, the 2's cognitivism, and the 3's social learning. Provide the participants with paper and colored markers. After they complete their drawings, have each person hold up their drawing and explain what it is and what it means.

6. Draw a large circle on the board or flip chart. Tell the participants that they are to create a pie chart with the pieces of the pie representing the strengths of their beliefs related to the three learning orientations. Draw an example that has three equal-sized pieces,

explaining that this would represent someone who believes equally in all three theories. Be careful not to make statements that imply right or wrong answers. Tell them that they can do this considering their beliefs in general, or they can focus on a very specific situation, for example, their beliefs when they were designing hands-on skill training for machinists. After the participants create their pie charts, ask if anyone would like to share their pie and the rationale for their decisions with the group.

7. Summarize the learning theory activities by having participants identify factors that might influence when one orientation might be more appropriate than another. As they describe the factors, write them on a flip chart with a column for Factors and a column for Learning Orientation.

8. Have participants spend 2 to 3 minutes individually thinking about current or upcoming situations in which they could apply this information about learning theories. Then have them divide into groups of three to discuss their action plans related to this topic. How do they think they are going to use this information on their jobs? What are they going to do differently as a result of this learning experience?

A good reference for background reading for this exercise is Merriam, S. B., and Caffarella, R. S. (1991) *Learning in Adulthood.* San Francisco: Jossey-Bass.

HOW PERCEPTIONS INFLUENCE BEHAVIOR: A DEMONSTRATION

Leslie Brunker

Leslie Brunker *is the originator of Unlimited Potentials Training and Consulting Services (6336 SE Milwaukie Avenue, Suite 26, Portland, OR 97202, 503-233-3859, liteup@fta.com). She has been an organizational consultant for fifteen years in the areas of interpersonal communication, conflict resolution, humor in the workplace, and team development. Leslie currently serves on the National Board of the North American Simulation and Gaming Association and the Columbia Northwest Chapter of the International Society for Performance Improvement.*

Overview This well-known exercise illustrates how individual behavior is influenced by the perceptions of others. It can also be used to show the impact of nonverbal communication. Finally, the exercise helps people begin to discover the interplay between the group and the individual.

Suggested Time 45 minutes.

Materials Needed ✓ 4 to 6 paper strips (approximately 30″ wide and 2″ high)
✓ Paper clips, tape, or glue (a way to join the ends of paper strips) to make headbands

Procedure 1. Make 4 to 6 paper headbands. Each headband will have a characteristic written on it. Select some from the list below or compose your own:

Clown	*Volatile*	*Controlling*
Withdrawn	*Powerful*	*Intelligent*
Friendly	*Creative*	*Competitive*
Whiner	*Doer*	*Pacifier*
Slacker	*Nurturer*	*Cooperative*

2. Introduce the exercise by discussing the power of perception. Post the expression: "Perception is everything." Ask participants to share ways in which the statement is true.

3. Select 4 to 6 volunteers from the group.

4. Form a "fishbowl" environment by putting the volunteers into the center while the observers surround them.

5. Randomly deal out the headbands, face down, to the volunteers in the center. Instruct them to *not* look at their headbands.

6. Have the volunteers attach each other's headbands so that they cannot see what is written on their own headband.

7. Assign the volunteer group a problem to discuss and solve that is relevant to this group's real-life situation, or you may make one up randomly, or select one from the examples listed below:

   ✓ They must decide whether to have a 5-day (8 hours/day) or 4-day (10 hours/day) week in their workplace.

   ✓ Their shipping time is four days and they must figure out a way to cut it in half.

   ✓ The communication between work teams has broken down and they must decide how to improve the process.

   ✓ Two people in their work group are always having a great deal of conflict and it is affecting the entire group. They must figure out a good, long-term solution.

   ✓ Two of the people in the work group like the temperature in the office to be cooler and two of the people like it to be warmer. This group must come up with a solution.

8. Instruct the volunteer group to engage in a discussion around the assigned problem. Tell them that they should treat each other according to the characteristics listed on their headbands, being careful not to reveal them.

9. Meanwhile, the outside group will observe and make note of incidents in the interactive process of the volunteer group. Allow the interaction to go on for at least ten minutes, long enough so that you see some behaviors change.

10. Stop the interaction and then first ask the volunteers to guess what they think their own cards say.

11. Debrief the exercise according to themes as listed in the section below.

Debriefing

When you debrief an exercise it is important to ask thought-provoking questions that allow people to make the connection from this exercise to the real world. You may want to focus your debriefing on a specific theme, or you may want to be more general. Here are some questions to help with the process of linking this exercise to the real world:

Questions for the Volunteer Group

How People Live Up to Expectations

How did you know what was expected of you?

How did you let others know what you expected?

When you didn't see the behavior you expected, what did you do?

What influences were the strongest in determining your behavior?

Nonverbal Communication

What nonverbal messages were you receiving from others?

What nonverbal messages were you sending to others?

How did you identify and interpret the messages you received?

What nonverbal messages influenced your behavior the most?

Which messages didn't influence your behavior? Why not?

The Group and the Individual

What did you notice about how others interacted with one another?

What kind of power influences were beginning to emerge?

Who had the most influence in this group? Why?

How did you try not to fit the characteristic that the group was trying to put you in?

Questions for the Observing Group

What dynamics did you observe in this process?

What were the signs that a person was being influenced by the group?

Were there things you wanted to say to this group as they were interacting?

What were they?

When did you perceive the characteristic expectations beginning to emerge?

What were the signs that the group was influencing the individuals' behavior?

How much power do you think we have as individuals to influence the group?

How can people effectively exercise their influence on a group?

From the external perspective, what advice would you give to those who are within a group?

13
THE WEAVER'S WEB: PRESENT AND FUTURE CONNECTIONS

Rima Shaffer

Rima Shaffer, *Ph.D. is the owner of Shaffer Synergistics (1303 Geranium Street NW, Washington, D.C. 20012, 202-291-9324), a consulting firm specializing in organization change, group decision making, self-directed work teams/cross-functional teams, the use of play to foster creativity and team building, and conflict resolution. Rima is also a core faculty member at Johns Hopkins University School of Applied Behavioral Sciences. She is a contributor to* **20 Active Training Programs,** *vol. III (Pfeiffer, in press).*

Overview Good training designs pay careful attention to endings. Well thought out endings help participants make the transition from the training event back to the workplace. They are also good beginnings that help participants discover ways of applying the training to the job and their lives. The purpose of this activity is to enable participants to graphically depict the synergy and connections that have developed during the workshop and to discover ways of building on this synergy. It works best for situations in which participants are not strangers to each other prior to the workshop.

Suggested Time 60 minutes.

Materials Needed ✓ A large ball of yarn
✓ A flip chart
✓ Markers
✓ Post-it-Notes®
✓ Tape

Procedure 1. Have participants stand and form a circle. Tell the group that often workshops are brought to a close without giving participants an opportunity to reflect on what they have learned, who they have connected with, or how they intend to use the material from the workshop on the job. The following exercise will help group members to create a web of connections that will extend beyond the workshop back to the job.

2. Ask one person to hold on to several inches from the end of the yarn and then throw the ball of yarn to another participant. Ask the participant to share some way in which s/he feels connected to the person she/he threw the yarn to. Participants will continue throwing the yarn to each other and stating how they are connected until each person has an opportunity to throw the yarn to all those she/he has established a strong connection to.

3. At the completion of this part of the exercise, have participants look at the web they have created. Have them note the connections that they have woven.

4. While the participants are still holding the yarn, ask them:
   ✓ What patterns and connections do you notice?
   ✓ How do these patterns and connections differ from the patterns that existed prior to the workshop?
   ✓ How are these patterns and connections similar to the patterns that existed prior to the workshop?

5. Go around the circle, and ask everyone to discuss what they notice and how they are feeling after having completed this part of the exercise. Expect that *participants generally note feelings of openness and connection. They may remark that these feelings are greater than those they normally experience on the job.*

6. End this part of the activity by having participants gently place the end of the yarn that they were holding on the floor and look at the floor pattern their web makes. Give each person a Post-it-Note®. Have them write their name on the Post-it-Note® and attach it to the bundle of strings s/he was holding.

7. Return participants to their seats and ask participants to create a list of factors that will enable them to build on and strengthen the connections they have made once they return to work. Record these factors on flip chart paper.

8. Have participants create a list of factors that will impede their ability to strengthen these connections when they return to work. *Note that these factors can be organizational or personal. Examples might include not having enough time to meet regularly or a reward system that discourages teamwork.* Record these factors on flip chart paper.

9. Invite participants to work with some of the people they selected when tossing the yarn. Instruct the groups to come up with ways they would like to work together back on the job. Have them pay particular attention to the steps they can take to support each other. Ask them to discuss what they can do to overcome some of the factors that will impede their ability to strengthen these connections on the job.

10. Have participants write their suggestions on Post-it-Notes® and post them on a wall. Then, ask participants to group the suggestions by category. (The group will be performing a content analysis.)

11. Have each participant place a check next to the group of suggestions that most captures their energy. Give participants time to meet with others who have identified the same group of suggestions as capturing their energy. Have the group plan next steps and report back to the full group. Have them answer the following questions:

   ✓ What are the next steps that must be taken to implement this group of suggestions?

   ✓ What roles will each person play to help implement this step?

   ✓ What must each person do to implement this suggestion?

   ✓ What support can each person offer?

   ✓ What will successful implementation of each step look like?

12. Conclude with these questions:

   ✓ How is everybody feeling?

   ✓ What new groupings have emerged for you?

   ✓ What is the most important thing that you can do to support another participant back on the job.

THANKS AND CONGRATULATIONS: A CLOSING ACTIVITY*

Bill Matthews

William R. Matthews *is a senior consultant/facilitator with Prism Performance Systems (37000 Grand River Ave., Suite 230, Farmington Hills, MI 48335, 810-474-8855, bmatt@msn.com), where he works with organizations from a variety of industries including automotive, healthcare, and financial. Bill's specialties include team, leadership, and organizational development, systemic change, facilitation skills, and educational games and simulations. He is a member of the board of directors of the North American Simulation and Gaming Association. Bill is also an adjunct lecturer in Education at The University of Michigan-Dearborn, and coauthor of the book,* **101 Ways to Jump Start Your Job Search** *(McGraw-Hill, 1996).*

Overview   Too often facilitators fail to spend as much time (and energy) on closing activities as they do on opening activities and icebreakers. From a content point of view, a *closer* can review, summarize, wrap up, and encourage application. From a people point of view, a closer can facilitate networking and leave-taking. This activity allows participants to recognize each others' contributions and personal development.

Suggested Time   30 minutes for a group of up to ten.

Materials Needed
✓ One #10 (business size) envelope per participant
✓ $(n - 1) \times n$ index cards [for a group of five, $(5 - 1) \times 5 = 20$ cards; 4 cards per participant]
✓ Pencils or pens
✓ A supply of postage stamps (optional)

Procedure   1. With a large group, divide the participants into approximately equal groups of six to eight. If the group is small, use a single group of up to ten.

---

*The author wishes to express his thanks to Sivasailam "Thiagi" Thiagarajan for his expert advice and friendly editing to help improve the delivery of this activity.

2. Give each participant a business size envelope and (n − 1) index cards. For example, if the group has five people, each participant gets one envelope and **four** cards.

3. Have each participant print his or her name on the address side of the envelope. When done, participants pass their envelopes to the person on the immediate right.

4. Ask each participant to read the name on the new envelope and to write that person a congratulatory note on one side of an index card and a thank you note on the other side of the card. After completing the card on both sides, the participant continues to pass the envelope to the right. Give this example:

> I receive an envelope with Tom's name on it. I write a note on the front of my first index card that says something like: *Congratulations on being the first person in the group to learn every group member's name. You have an excellent aptitude for names. An admirable quality in a trainer.*
>
> I turn the index card over and write another note that says: *Thank you for defending me when the other members of the team were verbally beating up on me. You are a very sensitive person.*

I place the completed card in the envelope marked "Tom" and pass it to the person on my right. In the meantime, I receive a new envelope with Nancy's name on it. I pick up my second index card and repeat the process just as before. I keep writing notes and passing envelopes along until I finally receive back the envelope with my own name on it. Now, I must decide if I want to read the contents right now, take it home with me to read, or complete my address on the front and mail it to myself for review at a later date.

5. It can be helpful to write some instructions on a flip chart or prepare an overhead, since the activity requires a number of mechanical steps. Instructions might read:

Write your name on envelope, pass it right and then:

✓ Receive an envelope, read name

✓ On index card, complete statement: *Thank you for …*

✓ On reverse, complete statement: *Congratulations on …*

✓ Insert card in envelope, *do not seal*

✓ Pass envelope right, receive new envelope, repeat process

6. Participants **may not** look at the previous note(s) inside the envelope. **Also, make sure you tell participants not to seal the envelope when they are done!**

7. The process stops when everyone receives his or her envelope back. Give each participant the choice to read the notes immediately or have them mailed for future review. Either way, encourage participants to take a few moments to guess what the notes may say before actually reading them.

ASSESSMENT INSTRUMENTS

In this section of *The 1997 McGraw-Hill Training and Performance Sourcebook*, you will find eight assessment instruments. With these instruments, you will be able to answer questions such as:

✓ How results-based are your training and development systems?

✓ How do you rate on the new management skills?

✓ Are your training materials instructionally sound?

✓ How confident are your managers in their abilities?

✓ Is training the right answer?

✓ How am I doing?

✓ Is computer-based training the right choice?

✓ What are your critical reflection skills?

The instruments are designed both to evaluate training/performance issues and to suggest areas for improvement. Most are not for research purposes. Instead, they are intended to build awareness, provide feedback about your own specific situation, and promote group reflection.

In selecting instruments for publication, a premium was placed on questionnaires or survey forms that are easy to understand and quick to complete. Preceding each instrument is an overview that contains the key questions to be assessed. The instrument itself is on a separate page(s) to make reproduction more convenient. All of the instruments are scorable and may contain guidelines for scoring interpretation. Some include questions for follow-up discussion.

Many of these instruments are ideal to utilize as activities in training sessions. Participants can complete the instrument you have selected prior to or during the session. After completion, ask participants to score and interpret their own results. Then, have them compare outcomes with other participants, either in pairs or in larger groupings. Be careful, however, to stress that the data from these instruments are not "hard." They *suggest* rather than *demonstrate* facts about people or situations. Ask participants to compare scores to their own perceptions. If they do not match, urge them to consider why. In some cases, the discrepancy may be due to the crudeness of the measurement device. In others, the discrepancy may result from distorted self-perceptions. Urge participants to open themselves to new feedback and awareness.

Other instruments will help you and others to assess future training needs. Again, it would be useful to show and discuss the data that emerges with others who are involved in the area under evaluation.

You may also wish to use some instruments as a basis for planning retreats or staff meetings. Have participants complete the instruments prior to the session. Then, summarize the results and open it up to team discussion.

If you choose this option, be sure to state the process clearly to respondents. You might want to use the following text:

We are planning to get together soon to identify issues that need to be worked through in order to maximize our future effectiveness. An excellent way to begin doing some of this work is to collect information through a questionnaire and to feed back that information for group discussion.

I would like you to join with your colleagues in filling out the attached questionnaire. Your honest responses will enable us to have a clear, objective view of our situation.

Your participation will be totally anonymous. My job will be to summarize the results and report them to the group for reaction.

You can also share the instruments with others in your organization who might find them useful for their own purposes. In some cases, merely reading through the questions is a valuable exercise in self and group reflection.

HOW RESULTS-BASED ARE YOUR TRAINING AND DEVELOPMENT PROGRAMS?

15

Jack Phillips

Jack J. Phillips, *Ph.D. has served in managerial and executive positions for over twenty-five years, including HRD manager and bank president. He is currently the president of Performance Resources Organization (P.O. Box 1969, Murfreesboro, TN 37133-1969, 615-896-7694), a consulting firm that provides human resource accountability services to a wide range of clients in ten countries. Jack has written or edited seven books and over 75 articles. He was also a contributor to* **The 1996 McGraw-Hill Team and Organization Development Sourcebook.**

OVERVIEW

Support is critical for the success of organization development, training and development, and human resource development programs. In most situations, the amount of support managers are willing to provide is directly linked to their perception of the effectiveness of the programs. If the programs are achieving results and help the organization to reach its goals, managers are often willing to support the programs by providing resources to make them successful, reinforcing specific behavioral objectives, and becoming more actively involved in the process.

The following instrument provides an assessment of the extent to which managers perceive that programs are achieving results. It provides the organization with an assessment of the effectiveness of training and development, human resource development, and organization development as perceived by the managers.

The assessment instrument can be used in the following ways:

✓ It can serve as a benchmark for specific efforts, events, and activities aimed at enhancing the level of support.

✓ It can serve as a periodic assessment of the progress made in the effort to increase the effectiveness of programs.

✓ It can serve as a useful discussion tool in workshops for managers where the goal is to enhance their support for the training or OD function.

✓ It is a helpful tool to compare one group of managers in a division, plant, region, or subsidiary company with others to determine where specific attention may be needed.

The target audience for the instrument is middle- and upper-level managers who are in the position to provide significant support to the training and development and organization development function. These are the key managers who can influence the success of those efforts.

This instrument should be administered without discussion. Participants and managers should be instructed to provide very candid responses. The results should be quickly tabulated by the respondents and discussed and interpreted as a group.

THE TRAINING AND DEVELOPMENT PROGRAM SURVEY

Directions: For each of the following statements, circle the response that best describes the Training and Development function at your organization. If none of the answers describe the situation, select the one that fits the best. Please be candid with your responses.

1. The direction of the Training and Development function at your organization:
   a. Shifts with requests, problems and changes as they occur.
   b. Is determined by Human Resources and adjusted as needed.
   c. Is based on a mission and strategic plan for the function.

2. The primary mode of operation of the Training and Development function is:
   a. To respond to requests by managers and other employees to deliver training programs and services.
   b. To help management react to crisis situations and reach solutions through training programs and services.
   c. To implement many training programs in collaboration with management to prevent problems and crisis situations.

3. The goals of the Training and Development function are:
   a. Set by the training staff based on perceived demand for programs.
   b. Developed consistent with human resources plans and goals.
   c. Developed to integrate with operating goals and strategic plans of the organization.

4. Most new programs are initiated:
   a. By request of top management.
   b. When a program appears to be successful in another organization.
   c. After a needs analysis has indicated that the program is needed.

5. When a major organizational change is made:
   a. We decide only which presentations are needed, not which skills are needed.
   b. We occasionally assess what new skills and knowledge are needed.
   c. We systematically evaluate what skills and knowledge are needed.

6. To define training plans:

   a. Management is asked to choose training from a list of "canned," existing courses.

   b. Employees are asked about their training needs.

   c. Training needs are systematically derived from a thorough analysis of performance problems.

7. When determining the timing of training and the target audiences:

   a. We have lengthy, nonspecific training courses for large audiences.

   b. We tie specific training needs to specific individuals and groups.

   c. We deliver training almost immediately before its use, and it is given only to those people who need it.

8. The responsibility for training results:

   a. Rests primarily with the training staff to ensure that the programs are successful.

   b. Is a responsibility of the training staff and line managers, who jointly ensure that results are obtained.

   c. Is a shared responsibility of the training staff, participants, and managers all working together to ensure success.

9. Systematic, objective evaluation designed to ensure that trainees are performing appropriately on the job:

   a. Is never accomplished. The only evaluations are during the program and they focus on how much the participants enjoyed the program.

   b. Is occasionally accomplished. Participants are asked if the training was effective on the job.

   c. Is frequently and systematically pursued. Performance is evaluated after training is completed.

10. New programs are developed:

    a. Internally, using a staff of instructional designers and specialists.

    b. By vendors. We usually purchase programs modified to meet the organization's needs.

    c. In the most economic and practical way to meet deadlines and cost objectives, using both internal staff and vendors.

11. Costs for training and OD are accumulated:

    a. On a total aggregate basis only.

    b. On a program by program basis.

    c. By specific process components such as development and delivery.

12. Management involvement in the training process is:

   a. Very low, with only occasional input.

   b. Moderate, usually by request or on an as-needed basis.

   c. Deliberately planned for all major training activities, to ensure a partnership arrangement.

13. To ensure that training is transferred into performance on the job, we:

   a. Encourage participants to apply what they have learned and report results.

   b. Ask managers to support and reinforce training and to report results.

   c. Utilize a variety of training transfer strategies appropriate for each situation.

14. The training staff's interaction with line management is:

   a. Rare. We almost never discuss issues with them.

   b. Occasional; during activities such as needs analysis or program coordination.

   c. Regular, to build relationships, as well as to develop and deliver programs.

15. Training and Development's role in major change efforts is:

   a. To conduct training to support the project, as required.

   b. To provide administrative support for the program, including training.

   c. To initiate the program, coordinate the overall effort, and measure its progress in addition to providing training.

16. Most managers view the Training and Development function as:

   a. A questionable function that wastes too much employee time.

   b. A necessary function that probably cannot be eliminated.

   c. An important resource that can be used to improve the organization.

17. Training and Development programs are:

   a. Subject-based. ("All supervisors attend the Performance Appraisal Workshop.")

   b. Individual results-based. ("The participant will reduce his or her error rate by at least 20%.")

   c. Organizational results-based. ("The cost of quality will decrease by 25%.")

18. The investment in Training and Development is measured primarily by:

   a. Subject opinions.

   b. Observations by management and reactions from participants.

   c. Dollar return through improved productivity, cost savings, or better quality.

19. The Training and Development effort consists of:

   a. Usually one-shot, seminar-type approaches.

   b. A full array of courses to meet individual needs.

   c. A variety of training and development programs implemented to bring about change in the organization.

20. New Training and Development programs are implemented at my organization without some formula method of evaluation:

   a. Regularly.

   b. Seldom.

   c. Never.

21. The results of training programs are communicated:

   a. When requested, to those who have a need to know.

   b. Occasionally, to members of management only.

   c. Routinely, to a variety of selected target audiences.

22. Management involvement in training evaluation:

   a. Is minor, with no specific responsibilities and few requests.

   b. Consists of informal responsibilities for evaluation, with some requests for formal training.

   c. Is very specific. All managers have some evaluation responsibilities.

23. During a business decline at my organization, the training function will:

   a. Be the first to have its staff reduced.

   b. Be retained at the same staffing level.

   c. Go untouched in staff reductions, and possibly even increase in staff size.

24. Budgeting for Training and Development is based on:

   a. Last year's budget.

   b. Whatever the training department can "sell."

   c. A zero-based system.

25. The principal group that must justify Training and Development expenditures is:

   a. The Training and Development department.

   b. The human resources or administrative function.

   c. Line management.

26. Over the last two years, the Training and Development budget as a percent of operating expenses has:

   a. Decreased.

   b. Remained stable.

   c. Increased.

27. Top management's involvement in the implementation of Training and Development programs:

   a. Is limited to sending invitations, extending congratulations, and passing out certificates.

   b. Includes monitoring progress, opening/closing speeches, and presenting information on the outlook of the organization.

   c. Includes program participation to see what's covered, conducting major segments of the program, and requiring key executives to be involved.

28. Line management involvement in conducting Training and Development programs is:

   a. Very minor; only HRD specialists conduct programs.

   b. Limited to a few specialists conducting programs in their areas of expertise.

   c. Significant. On the average, over half of the programs are conducted by key line managers.

29. When an employee completes a training program and returns to the job, his or her manager is likely to:

   a. Make no reference to the program.

   b. Ask questions about the program and encourage the use of the material.

   c. Require use of the program material and give positive rewards when the material is used successfully.

30. When an employee attends an outside seminar, upon return he or she is required to:

   a. Do nothing.

   b. Submit a report summarizing the program.

   c. Evaluate the seminar, outline plans for implementing the material covered, and estimate the value of the program.

Directions: Score the survey as follows. Allow:

1 point for each (a) response

3 points for each (b) response

5 points for each (c) response

Your total score will be between 30 and 150 points. Interpret your point total using the information below. The ranges are based on input from dozens of organizations and hundreds of managers.

Score Range	Score Analysis
120-150	**Outstanding** environment for achieving results using the Training and Development function. Great management support. A truly successful example of results-based Training and Development.
90-119	**Above Average** in achieving results with Training and Development. Good management support. A solid and methodical approach to results-based human resource management.
60-89	**Needs Improvement** to achieve desired results with Training and Development. Management support is ineffective. Training and Development programs do not usually focus on results.
30-59	**Serious Problems** with the success and status of Training and Development. Management support is nonexistent. Training and Development programs are not producing bottom-line results.

HOW DO YOU RATE ON THE NEW MANAGEMENT SKILLS?

16

Cynthia Solomon

Cynthia Solomon, *Ph.D. is a technical program specialist for FERMCO, an environmental restoration company in Ohio (6469 Fountains Blvd., West Chester, OH 45069, 513-777-5435). Cindy has led or designed organizational and professional development projects for her employer, the health care industry, and professional and private organizations. She authored* **TQM in Dietetics and Nutrition Services,** *and has designed several training and management documents. She also manages a private human resources development practice. Cynthia was a contributor to* **The 1996 McGraw-Hill Team and Organization Development Sourcebook.**

OVERVIEW

Management and business futurists are predicting that the successful manager in the not-so-distant future will have a different set of skills from the traditional manager of the twentieth century. Managers will resemble coaches and motivators, and will do things to help an empowered workforce be as successful and productive as they can be. This assessment instrument is designed for both you and your manager to rate you on your skills in view of those behaviors that are considered essential for the manager in the year 2000 and beyond. Use the scoring and interpretation sections to discover how to develop the most valuable management skills for the years ahead.

THE MANAGEMENT 2000 SURVEY

Rate the management skills of the person you are assessing using the following scale. Each statement MUST have a score assigned to it.

5 = Consistently
4 = Often
3 = Occasionally
2 = Infrequently
1 = Rarely or Never

_____ 1. Gives praise to employees and coworkers when they deserve it.

_____ 2. Uses informal memos and notes to get information out quickly.

_____ 3. Is willing to take a risk to try something different.

_____ 4. Considers the future of the organization when making decisions.

_____ 5. Takes the time to give helpful advice to an employee on a new assignment.

_____ 6. Lets employees know what areas of decisions they may make themselves.

_____ 7. Looks directly at people when being talked to.

_____ 8. Refuses to cover up mistakes to save face.

_____ 9. Stays with a project until it is done well.

_____ 10. Calls colleagues to obtain their expertise.

_____ 11. Gives new assignments as a reward for good work.

_____ 12. Circulates relevant documents to employees who might benefit from the information.

_____ 13. Realizes that others have different ideas, and that those ideas should be evaluated fairly.

_____ 14. Sees how work done today affects work that may be required tomorrow.

_____ 15. Advises more than directs.

_____ 16. Respects the decisions that teams make about how they will perform their work.

_____ 17. Invites input from all affected persons before making a decision.

_____ 18. Admits own mistakes and the mistakes of the department.

_____ 19. Is willing to give extra time to help others complete a task.

_____ 20. Involves representatives of other groups in planning work.

_____ 21. Expresses pleasure when work is well done.

_____ 22. Stops by employee's workstation to discuss the progress of work.

_____ 23. Recognizes and rewards creativity.

_____ 24. Plans for the future of the department.

_____ 25. Gives positive feedback to individuals and groups.

_____ 26. Supports skill development activities for employees.

_____ 27. Does not interrupt others when they are speaking.

_____ 28. Can be trusted with a confidence.

_____ 29. Speaks positively about the organization.

_____ 30. Invites people with different views to develop solutions to problems.

_____ 31. Recognizes accomplishment soon after it has been achieved.

_____ 32. Writes and speaks clearly so that what is meant is also what is understood.

_____ 33. Demonstrates a willingness to change.

_____ 34. Makes all department goals and expectations known to employees.

_____ 35. Helps individuals and groups identify options they could pursue.

_____ 36. Helps resolve conflict constructively and fairly.

_____ 37. Has an "open door policy" so employees know they can enter when they need to, and speak freely with no fear of reprisal.

_____ 38. Expects that all employees will be honest and ethical; sets an example.

_____ 39. Rebounds in a positive manner when there is a setback in work.

_____ 40. Considers how decisions made could affect other work groups.

Directions: Transfer your **self-assessment** scores from each survey question into the categories below. Total the scores for each category in the space provided.

Motivating	Communicating	Creating
1. _____	2. _____	3. _____
11. _____	12. _____	13. _____
21. _____	22. _____	23. _____
31. _____	32. _____	33. _____
Total:	Total:	Total:

Visioning	Coaching/Mentoring	Team Building
4. _____	5. _____	6. _____
14. _____	15. _____	16. _____
24. _____	25. _____	26. _____
34. _____	35. _____	36. _____
Total:	Total:	Total:

Listening	Trust Building	Committing
7. _____	8. _____	9. _____
17. _____	18. _____	19. _____
27. _____	28. _____	29. _____
37. _____	38. _____	39. _____
Total:	Total:	Total:

Collaborating

10. _____

20. _____

30. _____

40. _____

Total:

Directions: Transfer the scores from **your manager** to each survey question into the categories below. Total the scores for each category in the space provided.

Motivating

1. _____

11. _____

21. _____

31. _____

Total:

Communicating

2. _____

12. _____

22. _____

32. _____

Total:

Creating

3._____

13. _____

23. _____

33. _____

Total:

Visioning

4. _____

14. _____

24. _____

34. _____

Total:

Coaching/Mentoring

5. _____

15. _____

25. _____

35. _____

Total:

Team Building

6. _____

16. _____

26. _____

36. _____

Total:

Listening

7. _____

17. _____

27. _____

37. _____

Total:

Trust Building

8. _____

18. _____

28. _____

38. _____

Total:

Committing

9. _____

19. _____

29. _____

39. _____

Total:

Collaborating

10. _____

20. _____

30. _____

40. _____

Total:

Enter your self-assessment total for each management skill, as well as the scores from your manager.

Management Skills	Your Scores	Your Manager's Scores	Perception Difference (>2)
Motivating	_____	_____	_____
Communicating	_____	_____	_____
Creating	_____	_____	_____
Visioning	_____	_____	_____
Coaching/Mentoring	_____	_____	_____
Team Building	_____	_____	_____
Listening	_____	_____	_____
Trust Building	_____	_____	_____
Committing	_____	_____	_____
Collaborating	_____	_____	_____

✓ The ranges below indicate the frequency with which you and your manager perceive your use of the above management skills:

17-20	Very effective and consistent use
14-16	Effective use most of the time
11-13	Use of the skill, but it should be used more often
8-10	Insufficient demonstration of the skill
Below 8	Little or no demonstration of this skill

✓ Compare your personal score on each skill with the scores from your manager. If the difference between the two scores (for each skill) is greater than 2, you have a different perception of your skills as compared to your manager.

✓ Using the information gathered from both the survey scores and the differences in perception, determine what your strengths are and what skills you should develop for yourself. Create an action plan with your manager to help encourage the use of these skills in your daily work.

ARE YOUR TRAINING MATERIALS INSTRUCTIONALLY SOUND?

Susan Barksdale and Teri Lund

*Susan Barksdale is the founder of Front Line Evaluators (25-6 NW 23rd Place, #412, Portland, OR 97210, 503-223-7721), a training consulting firm specializing in evaluating training effectiveness. Susan provides return-on-investment evaluations for performance improvement initiatives and conducts instructional materials audits. **Teri Lund** is a partner in the firm Baldwin & Lund Services (4534 SW Tarlow Ct., Portland, OR 97221, 503-245-9020), which provides consultation in performance improvement methodologies for training professionals. Teri conducts return-on-investment evaluations and develops evaluation strategies for her clients.*

OVERVIEW

This assessment instrument, the Instructional Materials Audit Matrix, will assist you as you try to determine the effectiveness of your instructional materials. You can use this matrix either as a tool to evaluate instructional soundness "after the fact" or as a guideline for developing or purchasing new instructional materials.

Specific uses of this matrix include:

✓ *Strategic Planning*

Conduct an Instructional Materials Audit to determine the strengths, weaknesses, and gaps of existing curricula. Compare your findings to your organization's current business needs and decide if current courses will be maintained as is, modified, or deleted.

✓ *Preparing for Developing and Evaluating Requests for Proposals (RFPs)*

Use an audit to set the criteria for the design in the RFP to receive quality proposals that speak specifically to the desired results. Once you receive the proposals, conduct another audit to rate the response and sample materials.

✓ *Setting Standards for Internal and External Design and Development*

You can also use Instructional Materials Audits to identify and/or maintain instructional design and development standards. Use these standards both internally (within the department) or externally (with vendors) to assure consistency.

✓ *Validating Needs Assessment Findings*

Use the findings from an Instructional Materials Audit to validate needs assessments. An audit can also pinpoint areas within the curriculum that no longer meet the business need driving the training or performance improvement.

✓ *Procuring Off-the-Shelf Materials*

Identify design and development criteria by setting consistent standards when you purchase off-the-shelf materials. Communicate design and development expectations through the use of an audit when you make the decision to buy.

✓ *Providing a Structured Quality Improvement Process*

Use the Instructional Materials Audit to set standards for design and development as the basis of a structured quality improvement process. Judge current instructional materials against the standards as a baseline, set benchmarks for improvement, and then measure the progress to goals for all new development or procurement.

✓ *Developing a Maintenance Strategy*

Continuously monitor the effectiveness of the material design and development and compare the findings to current business and audience needs. An audit helps to develop a realistic and meaningful maintenance strategy that identifies what will be maintained, how it will be maintained, and what resources will be needed (financial, human, and material).

✓ *Managing Performance*

Use the identification of design and development criteria (as found in the audit matrix) to measure individual designer performance. Measuring progress to standards will reveal design and development strengths and weaknesses. Design and development skill gaps should be evident through the continuous use of audits.

INSTRUCTIONAL MATERIALS AUDIT MATRIX

Directions: The Instructional Materials Audit Matrix consists of four categories, each representing an important aspect of instructional design. These categories are:

✓ *General Information* such as name of module, type of training, methods of training, prerequisites, and audience.

✓ *Instructional Evaluation* including components such as outlines, objectives, sequencing, practice exercises, demonstration, and reinforcement.

✓ *Training Materials* including type of material/media provided, types of evaluations provided, directions, resource identification, and glossaries.

✓ *Training Evaluation/Effectiveness* such as coaching components, performance baselines, participant observation, and identified business needs.

Each of these categories contains subcategories that include the relevant assessment criteria.

To use this matrix, simply rate each criterion using a scale of 1 to 7 (1 = poor example of the criterion, 7 = a very good example of the criterion) and note this rating in the space provided. Make written comments in addition to using a numerical rating. This qualitative information will help support the quantitative ratings. Please note: The 1-7 rating scale is not applicable to the General Information Category.

CRITERIA	RATING	COMMENTS
General Information The first category of the audit matrix is titled "General Information." This section assesses components such as the type of training, the methods used in training, objectives, and audience. There are 9 items in this category.		
Name of Training/System The name of the training or the system.		
General Description of Content The content is described in general terms.		
Prerequisites Identified List prerequisites if they have been identified.		
Method of Training or Combination of Methods The training method(s) such as CBT, classroom, paper-based self-study, audio tape, etc.		
Audience/Targeted Instructional Group The targeted audience for the training.		
Length of Course or Program The time it will take to complete the training.		

CRITERIA	RATING	COMMENTS
Written or Customized for the Appropriate Industry The course or module was customized for the organization or the industry.		
Certification of Instructor Required Is certification of instructors required and if so how and by whom?		
Flexibility of Delivery Indicate the flexibility of delivery for individuals, small groups, large groups, and whether or not the materials are presented in modules or sections. Is the course limited to individuals or groups and what are the consequences of these limitations?		
Instructional Evaluation The second category of the audit matrix is "Instructional Evaluation." This category assesses items such as outlines, sequencing, practice exercises, and demonstrations of skills or knowledge. There are 9 items in this category.		
Lesson Plan/Course Outline Available A lesson plan or course or module outline is available. A lesson plan or course outline will describe the content of the course or module in detail.		

CRITERIA	RATING	COMMENTS
Learning Objectives/Goals of Training Are Outlined There are stated learning objectives that relate to the content and materials of the courseware.		
Design Is Consistent and Uniform There is a continuity and consistency to the design that is repeated throughout the course or module. Things to look for here include consistent use of icons, language, headers, footers, directions, exercises, etc.		
Desired Performance Is Described The expectations from completing the course or module are stated in behavioral terms that relate to the job learners are performing.		
Practice Exercise Relevant to Performance Expectations Is Provided Learning activities are embedded in the material that allow users an opportunity to assess their learning and to practice the skills that have been taught. Activities are provided frequently and appropriately to allow for relevant practice of new skills. This practice is related to job performance.		

CRITERIA	RATING	COMMENTS
Demonstration/Adequate Explanation of Knowledge-based Material Is Provided Materials provide a walk-through or demonstration of the steps to complete a task. Examples of this include: A video tape of a role play demonstrating the "right behaviors" or the system guiding the participant through screens and demonstrating how to complete fields.		
Training Reinforces Skills/Behavior through the Method(s) The method(s) of training supports and reinforces the skills learned and behaviors that are required on the job. For example, the CBT demonstrates appropriate dialogue that would take place between customers and claims representatives.		
A Testing/Post-training Evaluation Is Provided Learners are assessed on what they have learned or on their performance improvement. The data are tabulated and reported.		
Material Sequencing The materials are sequenced in a logical order and in a way that relates to the performance requirements of the job that is the object of the training.		

CRITERIA	RATING	COMMENTS
Training Materials The third category of the audit matrix is "Training Materials." This section assesses such components as type of materials provided, types of evaluations provided, directions, resource identifications, and glossaries. There are 10 items in this category.		
Program Specifications Document A design document or other high level documentation was reviewed and approved. This could also be CBT specs or a script concept document for the videos.		
Performance Evaluation Is Provided An evaluation of learner performance is included in materials, which provides feedback to learner about his or her transfer of knowledge and skills to on-the-job performance.		
Instructor/Leader's Guide Is Provided A leader's guide that outlines the course or module process and content is provided. This guide is important in ensuring consistency in delivery.		
Level 1 Evaluation Provided The effectiveness of the presentation is measured and analyzed. There is some type of evaluation or test of the content or a place for user input about the effectiveness.		

CRITERIA	RATING	COMMENTS
Realistic Cases/Exercises Are Provided Case studies and exercises are related to the learners' work environment and reflect realistic situations and problems.		
Directions Are Clear and Concise Directions for what the learner is to do in the course or module are clear. This is especially important in self-paced learning where the learner is working alone to complete the course.		
Materials/Design Support Active Participation or Interaction Participation and interaction are built into the training. This is important, regardless of method, as it leads to transfer to the job.		
Materials/Design Support Giving Feedback Feedback is built into the training and is provided by either the instructor or the learners.		
Application to Job Is Addressed Application to the job is addressed throughout the materials through relationships to performance requirements, examples, and exercises.		

CRITERIA	RATING	COMMENTS
Self-evaluation for Learner Is Provided The learner is able to evaluate progress in understanding and applying the course or module content. This is done through discussions (if classroom), self-assessments, written exercises, demonstrations, and skill practices.		
Training Evaluation/Effectiveness The fourth category of the audit matrix is "Training Evaluation/Effectiveness." This category contains components such as coaching, performance baselines, business need identified. There are 10 items in this category.		
Coaching Component Is Provided The process of improving task performance by providing detailed demonstration, frequent practice, and both corrective and motivational feedback is provided in exercises or formalized observations back on the job.		
Demonstrates Increased Employee Effectiveness/Development Employees are formally assessed through observation or other assessments to determine an increase in either their effectiveness in tasks or development of behaviors or skills in general. Normally, baselining is required to measure this increase.		

CRITERIA	RATING	COMMENTS
Demonstrates Increased Business Unit Profits Specific business impact is identified as a result of this intervention—such as an increase in sales. Specific work measures are reviewed to verify an increase in business unit profit or a decrease in costs has occurred post-training or intervention.		
Participants Are Observed in Their Work Environment and Given Feedback to Improve Skills/Behaviors There is a formal process designed and discussed that initiates observation, feedback, and reinforcement of skills and behavior back on the job. This is communicated in the materials and the course design promotes the process.		
Participants Are Tested to Measure an Increase in Knowledge Participants are assessed against precise, measurable performance criteria and must demonstrate the behavior, skills, or knowledge in order to prove a targeted competency level. (A baseline test should be provided.)		
Post-training Evaluation Provided Participants are provided with a post-training evaluation in one or more of the following time frames: 30 days; 60 days; 90 days; 120 days.		

CRITERIA	RATING	COMMENTS
This evaluation requests information regarding the applicability of the training back to the job, if the participants are using what they learned, and what performance barriers exist to utilizing the information or skills to the fullest extent.		
Training Results Are Tracked and Reported at Class Level or Participant Level Training results are reported at a class or participant level by mastery of items or competencies. Information is usually tracked for no-shows, those who canceled, or those who completed only part of the training. This tracking may be completed manually or through an automated method.		
Business Need Is Identified and Presented in Materials The business need is clearly explained in the material as to why this training is being undertaken, and is tied to the desired performance of the participants.		
Performance Expectations Are Clearly Communicated Behaviors, skills, and knowledge expected as a result of the training are clearly explained to learners in the materials.		

CRITERIA	RATING	COMMENTS
Expected Business Results Are Identified and Communicated Business results such as decreases in costs, increased member satisfaction, less rework, increased sales are clearly identified as learner expectations in the training materials.		

SCORING THE INSTRUCTIONAL MATERIALS AUDIT MATRIX

It is important for you to preestablish the value of the rating scale when using this audit matrix. These values are highly dependent on the reason the audit is being conducted and the way in which the results will be used. For example, when using these criteria to assess a vendor's ability to design and develop a training program, assign points to each criterion and total them at the completion of the assessment. In this case, because you are making a comparison, the higher the number of points, the more instructionally sound the vendor materials and therefore, the better able the vendor should be in meeting your design need. If you are conducting a design audit to discover the strengths, weaknesses, and gaps of a current curriculum, you will most likely not add point values because you are comparing the program only to itself. In this case, the 1 to 7 ratings with descriptive comments are sufficient.

HOW CONFIDENT ARE YOUR MANAGERS IN THEIR ABILITIES?

18

Phil Donnison

Philip Donnison *is course director and training consultant at Brathay Development Training (Brathay Hall, Ambleside, Cumbria, LA22 0HP, England, UK (+44) 015394 33041, pdonnison@kendal.compulink.co.uk), an outdoor management development provider in the UK. He works with senior managers and strategic teams and specializes in experiential learning, personal development, and the facilitation of senior teams. Phil is a Chartered Occupational Psychologist.*

OVERVIEW

This instrument identifies the specific beliefs people have about their managerial abilities. The beliefs people hold about their abilities are major determinants of their behavior.

Training programs may teach new knowledge, skills, and capabilities. However, the acquisition of knowledge and skills is not enough for a fully accomplished performance. A person may know what to do, but may not feel able to do it. Only by having a degree of self-efficacy (the belief that one can successfully perform a given behavior in a given situation) around the task will a person be able to perform.

The *Managerial Tasks Questionnaire* measures first line managers' self-efficacy by assessing their confidence to succeed at each of the specific tasks that make up their jobs. The results from the instrument provide feedback on the extent to which managers feel able to apply the knowledge and skills they have acquired during a training program.

Use the survey to assess how confident managers feel about each or all of the tasks that make up their jobs. Or, use it as a way to assess the impact of training on their capabilities or to diagnose training needs. The survey can also be used to evaluate the effectiveness of a training event (it can be administered before and after and to a control group for comparison).

The questionnaire was designed specifically for first-line managers and supervisors by using a specific research framework with a group of line managers. If the descriptions are appropriate the questionnaire can be used "off-the-shelf." Alternatively, it can be also be adapted to include only those task descriptions that are relevant.

The *Managerial Tasks Questionnaire* contains descriptions of 30 tasks. Respondents are asked to indicate how confident they feel about their ability to carry out each task. The total score gives an indication of an individual's self-efficacy for the tasks that make up a job. Scores for each task allow diagnosis of any specific areas in which they do not feel confident.

THE MANAGERIAL TASKS QUESTIONNAIRE

Please indicate your confidence in your ability to carry out each task listed below by circling the appropriate number in the right-hand column.

Task	Confidence 1 (not confident) 10 (completely confident)
1. Planning and scheduling the work activities of the department.	1 2 3 4 5 6 7 8 9 10
2. Allocating and controlling use of available resources.	1 2 3 4 5 6 7 8 9 10
3. Conducting performance appraisal interviews with staff.	1 2 3 4 5 6 7 8 9 10
4. Monitoring the performance of staff.	1 2 3 4 5 6 7 8 9 10
5. Setting goals to achieve the objectives for the unit.	1 2 3 4 5 6 7 8 9 10
6. Using disciplinary procedures with staff.	1 2 3 4 5 6 7 8 9 10
7. Delegating/allocating work to staff.	1 2 3 4 5 6 7 8 9 10
8. Negotiating to achieve your aims.	1 2 3 4 5 6 7 8 9 10
9. Solving problems in a creative way.	1 2 3 4 5 6 7 8 9 10
10. Analyzing management information and statistics.	1 2 3 4 5 6 7 8 9 10
11. Counseling staff who have problems.	1 2 3 4 5 6 7 8 9 10
12. Playing an active part in meetings.	1 2 3 4 5 6 7 8 9 10
13. Managing projects.	1 2 3 4 5 6 7 8 9 10
14. Reviewing and improving work procedures.	1 2 3 4 5 6 7 8 9 10
15. Managing your own time.	1 2 3 4 5 6 7 8 9 10
16. Organizing the work of the unit.	1 2 3 4 5 6 7 8 9 10
17. Acting as a source of technical knowledge.	1 2 3 4 5 6 7 8 9 10
18. Checking that work has been completed to a standard.	1 2 3 4 5 6 7 8 9 10
19. Liaising with customers/external staff.	1 2 3 4 5 6 7 8 9 10
20. Interviewing potential new hires.	1 2 3 4 5 6 7 8 9 10
21. Encouraging staff to work as a team.	1 2 3 4 5 6 7 8 9 10
22. Developing staff through training and coaching.	1 2 3 4 5 6 7 8 9 10
23. Leading staff by setting standards.	1 2 3 4 5 6 7 8 9 10
24. Motivating and encouraging staff to achieve goals.	1 2 3 4 5 6 7 8 9 10
25. Communicating information to and from staff.	1 2 3 4 5 6 7 8 9 10
26. Maintaining standards of quality of work.	1 2 3 4 5 6 7 8 9 10
27. Supervising staff.	1 2 3 4 5 6 7 8 9 10
28. Making decisions.	1 2 3 4 5 6 7 8 9 10
29. Writing reports, memos, etc.	1 2 3 4 5 6 7 8 9 10
30. Giving presentations.	1 2 3 4 5 6 7 8 9 10

The scores for each of the 30 tasks can be added together to give an overall self-efficacy score for the manager's confidence in ability to carry out the tasks. Alternatively, the score for each task could be analyzed to identify those areas for further development for the individual.

The instrument can also be used with a group of managers to identify the average score for each task. This will build up a picture of the task areas that could be the target for management development for the group.

19 IS TRAINING THE RIGHT ANSWER?

Roger Chevalier

Roger Chevalier, *Ph.D. is a principal in the Performance Systems Group (924 Hudis Street, Rohnert Park, CA 94928, 707-584-7160), a management consulting organization specializing in the design and installation of management and sales systems. He is also an affiliate of the Center for Leadership Studies.*

OVERVIEW

The assessment instrument that follows guides the process of defining a performance shortfall and systematically analyzing the potential causes. Based on force field analysis and systems analysis, the instrument produces a clear picture of the underlying causes from which an improvement strategy can be easily derived.

Typically, trainers' involvement used to begin when a line manager requested a course to solve a problem that was less than clearly defined. The manager felt "pain" and looked upon training as a "quick fix" to the problem. Using that scenario, all trainers had to do was design and present classroom training. Then someone asked about measuring the effectiveness of the training provided. Next came the push for greater efficiency. Now comes the frequently asked question: "Is training really the solution we need?"

The most expensive way to solve a performance discrepancy is through classroom training. The costs, which include instructor salaries, student salaries, travel expenses, course development resources, and classroom upkeep, are enormous. What makes the situation worse is that the training may not be effective, particularly if the work environment does not support the skills and procedures we have just trained. To the line manager, the benefits may not be worth the costs.

Whether the problem is poor productivity, quality, cost overruns, poor employee morale, or customer dissatisfaction, the first step is to identify the cause. There are many questions to ask. Is it a lack of knowledge or skills? Were the employees properly selected? Is the job properly designed? Is it a lack of employee motivation and goal alignment? Does the reward system reinforce the appropriate goals? Do standard operating procedures exist? The *Performance Discrepancy Analysis Worksheet* will help you to determine the root cause of the problem and explore possible performance solutions.

PERFORMANCE DISCREPANCY ANALYSIS WORKSHEET

Where we are: _____

Where we want to be: _____

Factors	Driving Forces					Restraining Forces			
	+4	+3	+2	+1	0	−1	−2	−3	−4
human/social									
knowledge	•	•	•	•		•	•	•	•
skills	•	•	•	•		•	•	•	•
motivation	•	•	•	•		•	•	•	•
reward systems	•	•	•	•		•	•	•	•
group norms	•	•	•	•		•	•	•	•
informal leaders	•	•	•	•		•	•	•	•
political climate	•	•	•	•		•	•	•	•
technical									
job design	•	•	•	•		•	•	•	•
tools/equipment	•	•	•	•		•	•	•	•
procedures	•	•	•	•		•	•	•	•
technology	•	•	•	•		•	•	•	•
information									
goals/objectives	•	•	•	•		•	•	•	•
measurement	•	•	•	•		•	•	•	•
data/information	•	•	•	•		•	•	•	•
filtering	•	•	•	•		•	•	•	•
decision makers	•	•	•	•		•	•	•	•
suboptimization	•	•	•	•		•	•	•	•
structural									
organization	•	•	•	•		•	•	•	•
control systems	•	•	•	•		•	•	•	•
flexibility	•	•	•	•		•	•	•	•
feedback	•	•	•	•		•	•	•	•
clear roles	•	•	•	•		•	•	•	•

1. Begin the analysis process by having line managers define the performance discrepancy in terms of "where we are" (the present level of performance), and "where we want to be" (the desired level of performance). After setting these end points in highly measurable terms including quantity, quality, time, and cost, identify and evaluate the relative importance of the forces working for (driving forces) and against (restraining forces) the resolution of the problem.

   Example:

   You are working with the vice president of sales who has requested a three-day course to improve the performance of her salespeople. With your help she defines the problem as:

   Where we are: <u>*A talented but complacent sales force achieving only 70% of their performance goals.*</u>

   Where we want to be: <u>*A motivated sales force that meets or exceeds all performance goals.*</u>

   With your assistance she describes her salespeople as being very knowledgeable and reasonably skilled but unmotivated. While the commission plan does reward some performance goals, it misses the mark on many others. The salespeople often band together to resist management decisions and have strong informal leaders that are working against performance. The political climate is negative, and reorganizations and layoffs are routine.

2. Use the Performance Discrepancy Analysis Worksheet to guide your analysis of the performance problem through the human/social, technical, information and structural subsystems of your organization. Analyze these comments and evaluate the strength of each factor on a 1 to 4 scale. By clearly identifying and displaying the driving and restraining forces, the line manager is in a much better position to deal with the problem. Creative solutions are found in adding to or strengthening driving forces while removing or weakening restraining forces.

   Example:

	Driving Forces					Restraining Forces			
	+4	+3	+2	+1	0	–1	–2	–3	–4
knowledge	•	→→→→→→→				•	•	•	•
skills	•	•	→→→→→			•	•	•	•
motivation	•	•	•	•	←←←←←←←			•	•
reward systems	•	•	→→→→→			•	•	•	•
group norms	•	•	•	•	←←←←←←←←←←←				•
informal leaders	•	•	•	•	←←←←←←←←←			•	•
political climate	•	•	→→→→→			•	•	•	•

The worksheet that you've just completed should help you to determine if training really is the best solution for resolving a performance discrepancy problem. Training may be part of the solution if there is a need for new knowledge or skills. But for the other potential problem areas, training will not help to close the gap between "where we are" and "where we want to be."

Training is not the solution for other human/social subsystem factors such as a lack of desire to perform, reward systems that do not reinforce goals, norms and informal leaders that are working against management, or a political climate that restricts performance. Nor will training correct technical subsystem factors such as poorly designed jobs, lack of needed tools or procedures, or rapid changes in technology.

Similarly, training will do little in the information/decision making subsystems to correct poorly defined goals, lack of clear performance measures or usable information, remote decision makers, or suboptimization of resources. Nor will training resolve poor organizational structure, lack of control systems, lack of flexibility, ineffective feedback mechanisms, or overlapping of roles and responsibilities.

Classroom training is not the best alternative for most of the problem areas described above. Less expensive and potentially more effective alternatives to training include the development of clear organizational goals and structures as well as standards of performance with appropriate reward/sanction systems. Your recommendations may also include greater employee involvement to capture their ideas and motivation.

While training is "the drug of choice" to alleviate pain within many organizations, proper analysis of the performance discrepancy may reveal more efficient and effective ways to improve performance.

HOW AM I DOING?

Don Conover

Donald K. Conover *(2171 Twining Road, Newtown, PA 18940, 215-968-0608) is retired from AT&T where he had been the Corporate Education and Training Vice President. He is author of the chapter on leadership in the newly published 4th edition of the* **ASTD Training & Development Handbook** *(McGraw-Hill, 1996.) Don is active in the Chamber of Commerce and Rotary Club of Princeton and serves on the Board of Directors of the Thomas Edison State College Foundation.*

OVERVIEW

In the 1990's, most people work in an organization that is in the process of transforming itself, redirecting its priorities, reorganizing its resources, and coping with accelerating change. In these conditions, five core values have emerged that underlie anyone's performance, be they a starting grade clerk or the vice president of the whole organization:

✓ respect for individuals

✓ dedication to helping customers

✓ highest standards of integrity

✓ innovation

✓ teamwork

The *Personal Development Feedback Form* is a 360-degree survey designed to assess how well an individual applies these core values in daily tasks. It may be understood best as a "personal market study"—how a person is impacting on the people he or she serves.

THE PERSONAL DEVELOPMENT FEEDBACK FORM

This is a survey you can use to obtain feedback from anybody who sees you perform your job. Begin by selecting your own sample of associates, including coworkers, supervisors, direct reports, customers, or suppliers. Contact them and request that they complete the survey. If you wish to put your request in writing, here is a sample text:

Jane Doe,

I am currently engaged in a process that provides me with perspectives about the way my actions on the job are perceived by others. One of the ways this goal is to be achieved is to receive feedback on how I apply five core values in my job: respect for individuals, dedication to helping customers, standards of integrity, innovation, and teamwork.

To this end, I have selected people with whom I work to send a copy of The Personal Development Feedback survey. You are among those I have selected to assess my effectiveness in the five key areas.

The survey is only one side of one page and should take less than 5 minutes to complete. Once you have finished the survey, return it to _____ (specify a third party). Your responses and those of others in my sample will be returned to me as summarized results. The information summary I receive will not reveal how you or any other individual in my sample responds.

Your timely response is valuable to me. The fact that I have selected you to complete this survey indicates my confidence in your candid and forthright feedback.

John Doe

Arrange for a third party to receive the surveys and aggregate the responses. The results should be formatted like a copy of the survey. The number represents how many of your evaluators rated you "consistent," "often," etc. for each question.

PERSONAL DEVELOPMENT FEEDBACK FOR:

(Name) _____

RESPECT FOR INDIVIDUALS:

1. Treats others with respect and dignity, valuing individual and cultural differences
   ❏ consistently ❏ usually ❏ often ❏ sometimes ❏ seldom

2. Communicates frequently and with candor
   ❏ consistently ❏ usually ❏ often ❏ sometimes ❏ seldom

3. Listens to others, without regard for level or position
   ❏ consistently ❏ usually ❏ often ❏ sometimes ❏ seldom

4. Gives individuals the authority to use their capabilities
   ❏ consistently ❏ usually ❏ often ❏ sometimes ❏ seldom

5. Supports continuous learning and personal growth
   ❏ consistently ❏ usually ❏ often ❏ sometimes ❏ seldom

DEDICATION TO HELPING CUSTOMERS:

1. Demonstrates care for customers and builds enduring relationships
   ❏ consistently ❏ usually ❏ often ❏ sometimes ❏ seldom

2. Anticipates and responds to customers' needs
   ❏ consistently ❏ usually ❏ often ❏ sometimes ❏ seldom

3. Delivers superior products and services
   ❏ consistently ❏ usually ❏ often ❏ sometimes ❏ seldom

HIGHEST STANDARD OF INTEGRITY:

1. Is honest and ethical in business and personal conduct
   ❏ consistently ❏ usually ❏ often ❏ sometimes ❏ seldom

2. Builds trust by keeping promises and admitting mistakes
   ❏ consistently ❏ usually ❏ often ❏ sometimes ❏ seldom

INNOVATION:

1. Encourages creativity
   - ❏ consistently ❏ usually ❏ often ❏ sometimes ❏ seldom
2. Seeks different perspectives
   - ❏ consistently ❏ usually ❏ often ❏ sometimes ❏ seldom
3. Takes risks by pursuing new opportunities
   - ❏ consistently ❏ usually ❏ often ❏ sometimes ❏ seldom

TEAMWORK:

1. Encourages and rewards both individual and team achievements
   - ❏ consistently ❏ usually ❏ often ❏ sometimes ❏ seldom
2. Cooperates across organizational boundaries
   - ❏ consistently ❏ usually ❏ often ❏ sometimes ❏ seldom
3. Extends team spirit through involvement in the community at large
   - ❏ consistently ❏ usually ❏ often ❏ sometimes ❏ seldom

INTERPRETING THE PERSONAL DEVELOPMENT FEEDBACK FORM

Here are some recommendations when reviewing the results of The Personal Development Feedback Form:

✓ Assess yourself on The Personal Development Feedback Form and compare your perceptions to the perceptions of others.

✓ Examine how consistent the results are. Do others see you in the same way? If there are a variety of perceptions, ask yourself why that may be.

✓ Discuss the results with a person who might be helpful in clarifying the feedback and identifying new behaviors that will better your commitment to the core values assessed in The Personal Development Feedback Form.

✓ Talk directly with the individual respondents, asking them for more specific feedback about behaviors to avoid or enhance.

✓ Create a self-development plan that furthers your personal growth as an individual working in the challenging environment of the 1990's.

✓ If done on an organizational basis, aggregate the total responses and compare your scores to those. See how you fare against a local benchmark.

IS COMPUTER-BASED TRAINING THE RIGHT CHOICE?

Nina Adams

Nina Adams *is the president of the Adams Consulting Group (3952 Western Ave., Western Springs, IL 60558, 708-246-0766, ninaa@mcs.com), specialists in training and marketing applications using interactive multimedia and virtual reality. She has twenty-five years' experience as a project manager, virtual reality designer, systems analyst, instructional designer, systems engineer, and workshop facilitator. Nina has also published articles about computer-based training, media selection, and virtual reality.*

OVERVIEW

Having trouble deciding whether or not your organization should invest in a computer-based training system? Use this assessment instrument to do a thorough analysis before you spend valuable time and effort investing in CBT. The instrument details twenty-seven criteria by which you can judge whether or not your next training project should be computer-based.

Divided into two sections, Learning and Corporate Issues, the Computer-based Training Decision Aid is structured in such a way as to encompass a wide variety of criteria and considerations that might affect the success and value of a computer-based training project. You may want to change some of the point values for each consideration to reflect your own organization's circumstances. For instance, if management's past experience with CBT has been very negative, you might subtract points for that consideration rather than merely assigning no points, as the guide suggests. If you change point values, however, remember to compensate before making any decisions based on the final totals.

COMPUTER-BASED TRAINING DECISION AID

Instructions: Write in a number value in the column "Actual Points" for each of the criteria listed. Subtotal your responses to each of the two sections and add them together to arrive at a total valuation of your computer-based training project.

LEARNING ISSUES

Criteria	Considerations	Possible Points	Actual Points
1. Number of learners.	If fewer than 50 50 to 100 More than 100	0 5 10	

2. Number of preferred training sites.	If learners are at
	  One site
	  One to five sites
	  More than five sites
		0
		5
		10	

3. Distance of learners from existing training site.	If bringing the average learner to the training site
	  Does not require overnight stay
	  Does require overnight stay
	  Requires many overnight stays
		0
		5
		10	

4. Number of times program will be offered.	Once Two to five times Six to 19 times 20 times or more	0 3 5 10	

5. Frequency of updates.	If changes/updates are needed
	  Every three months or less
	  Between three and six months
	  6 months or more
		0
		5
		10	

6. Development time available.	If training must be available in
	  Less than three months
	  Three to six months
	  Six months or more
		0
		5
		10	

7. Preferred learning style.	If learners prefer
	  Group learning
	  Independent learning
		0
		10	

8. Preferred training schedule.	If it is more appropriate to
	  Set training schedules
	  Allow learners to set schedules
		3
		10	

Criteria	Considerations	Possible Points	Actual Points
9. Current computer proficiency.	If learners Don't know how to use a computer and don't need a computer for their jobs Don't know how to use a computer and do need a computer for their jobs Know how to use a computer	0 5 10	
10. Current learner skill level.	If learners All have the same skill level Have widely varying skill levels	5 10	
11. Need for individualized remediation.	If learners probably Won't need remediation Will need remediation	5 10	
12. Importance of consistency.	If consistency is Not important Somewhat important Very important	0 5 10	
13. Need for performance tracking.	If performance tracking across multiple courses or modules is Not needed Desirable Required	0 5 10	
14. Content.	If skills are Interpersonal Technical	5 10	
15. Content already available on CBT.	If CBT program Must be developed to meet requirements Can be purchased and modified to meet requirements Can be purchased for use without modification	0 5 10	

Learning Issues Subtotal ———

Criteria	Considerations	Possible Points	Actual Points
16. Management's past experience with CBT.	If past experience with CBT was		
	Not favorable	0	
	Neutral	5	
	Very favorable	10	
17. General view of technology.	If management views technology as		
	Awful	0	
	A necessary evil	5	
	Great	10	
18. Budgeting scheme.	For cost comparisons, if development costs		
	Are separated from costs of delivery	0	
	Are included with delivery costs	10	
19. Availability of hardware at learner site.	If hardware at learner site is		
	Not available at all	0	
	Available but has to be upgraded	5	
	Available	10	
20. Cash flow.	If cash flow is		
	Slow	0	
	OK	5	
	Good	10	
21. Management's perception of person making recommendation.	If person making recommendation		
	Has a poor track record	0	
	Has a great track record	10	
22. Availability and skills of project management staff.	If staff can		
	Not manage a CBT project	0	
	Manage project	10	
23. Availability of production hardware.	If production hardware is		
	Not available at all	0	
	Available but has to be upgraded	5	
	Not needed	10	
	Available	10	

Criteria	Considerations	Possible Points	Actual Points
24. Availability and knowledge of CBT design and authoring.	If staff Does not know anything about authoring Will buy off the shelf CBT Can design and author CBT language.	0 5 10	
25. Availability of hardware troubleshooters.	If troubleshooters Cannot be made available Can be made available	0 10	
26. Availability of content experts.	If content questions must be answered and experts Cannot be made available Can be made available	0 10	
27. Use of existing trainers.	If existing trainers Will no longer be needed Can be transferred to new positions Can be used on CBT projects	0 5 10	

Subtotal for Corporate Issues _____

GRAND TOTAL _____

INTERPRETING THE COMPUTER-BASED TRAINING
DECISION AID

If your grand total is less than 135, CBT is not an appropriate fit for this particular training project. A total in the range of 135 to 200 points indicates that CBT is a viable option. If your grand total is over 200 points, a computer-based training program is probably the right choice.

HOW ARE YOUR CRITICAL REFLECTION SKILLS?

22

Francesco Sofo

Francesco Sofo, *Ph.D. is an academic and consultant in Adult Education/Human Resource Development at the University of Canberra (P.O. Box 1 Belconnen, ACT 2616, Australia, 616-2015123, franks@education.canberra.edu.au). Formerly chair of the HRD/Adult Education Program and Founding Director of the Center for HRD Studies, he is currently senior lecturer and convenor of the Masters in Community Education (HRD) Program. He is the author of* **Critical Reflection Strategies Using Teams** *(1995) and lead author of* **The Critical Reflection Inventory (CRI) Self-Rating Scales Manual** *(1996).*

OVERVIEW

This assessment instrument measures your perceptions of your critical reflection skills. What are the dimensions of critical reflection? They are identified in this instrument as follows:

Dimensions of Critical Reflection	Abbreviation
Differences	DI
Non-Personalization	NP
Empathy	EM
Observation	OB
Cognitive Awareness	CA
Openness	OP

Why is critical reflection important? Being critically reflective is a very powerful mechanism in adult learning for making change happen. You can become critically reflective of the content of a problem or a process, and also be critically reflective of how you solve a problem or how a problem is framed in the first place. We change our points of view by becoming critically reflective of the content and the process of problem solving. The way we change our mental habits is to become critically reflective of the premises of a problem.

There are two ways of becoming critically reflective: by objective or subjective reframing. If you are reading something and you ask about the assumptions of the author, you are asking about assumptions outside yourself. This is being critically reflective, also termed objective reframing.

Subjective reframing is when you become critically reflective of your own assumptions and your own frame of reference. It is when you ask yourself, "How did I fall into the habit of thinking a certain way?" This is the most potentially powerful learning experience of adulthood. Essentially people are encouraged to become critically reflective of assumptions that they've previously taken for granted. This is very empowering.

The Critical Reflection Inventory is designed to help people improve their critical reflection abilities by raising their own awareness of themselves and discussing their own profiles. This inventory measures people's perceptions of their critical thinking skills and summarizes the results into six dimensions of critical reflection. You can both take and score the CRI within ten minutes. Respondents read each of the 24 statements and circle the number that most accurately matches current behavior using a Likert scale ranging from 1 to 6. It is desirable to have skills in all six of the critical reflection dimensions measured in this inventory. More detailed scoring instructions are listed after the inventory itself.

THE CRITICAL REFLECTION INVENTORY (CRI)*

DIRECTIONS: Following is a list of statements about critical reflection. Read each statement and circle the number that most accurately matches your current behavior. A rating of 1 indicates that the statement is very undescriptive of your current behavior, while a rating of 6 indicates that you frequently behave in the manner described.

1. I do not mind when a person that I'm solving problems with has different values from my own.   1 2 3 4 5 6

2. I become anxious if someone opposes my views.   1 2 3 4 5 6

3. I am sensitive to the feelings of others.   1 2 3 4 5 6

4. My observations are accurate.   1 2 3 4 5 6

5. I make impulsive decisions.   1 2 3 4 5 6

6. I am open-minded.   1 2 3 4 5 6

7. I evaluate the pros and cons of different options when I solve problems.   1 2 3 4 5 6

8. I feel attacked when others present opinions that are different from my own.   1 2 3 4 5 6

9. I can sense when others have strong reactions.   1 2 3 4 5 6

10. I notice my own way of thinking as a way of making my thinking more accurate.   1 2 3 4 5 6

11. I think carefully about problems rather than acting on impulse.   1 2 3 4 5 6

12. I monitor my feelings when I address an issue.   1 2 3 4 5 6

*Adapted from Sofo, Francesco, and Kendall, Lawrence. (1996) *The Critical Reflection Inventory (CRI) Self-Rating Scales: Forms A, B & C Manual.* F & M Sofo Educational Assistance. 55 Vagabond Cr. McKELLAR, 2617 ACT, Australia. ISBN 0-646-291793.

13. I am sensitive to others' ideas.   1 2 3 4 5 6

14. I am afraid to bring conflicting points of   1 2 3 4 5 6
view out into the open.

15. I am good at making sense of behavior.   1 2 3 4 5 6

16. I have different ways of observing the   1 2 3 4 5 6
same situation.

17. I know when others are confused.   1 2 3 4 5 6

18. I refuse to change my beliefs even if I find   1 2 3 4 5 6
that they are not worthwhile.

19. I can understand other people's   1 2 3 4 5 6
perspectives.

20. I become defensive when others reject   1 2 3 4 5 6
my ideas.

21. I am aware of my biases when I make   1 2 3 4 5 6
observations.

22. I can describe many facets of what   1 2 3 4 5 6
I observe.

23. I have noticed myself shifting toward a   1 2 3 4 5 6
more open-minded perspective.

24. I question my own assumptions.   1 2 3 4 5 6

Note that the items marked with an "R" are REVERSED items. This means that where a score of 6 has been circled on that item in the inventory, then the number 1 is scored for that item. Where a 1 has been circled in the inventory then a 6 is scored. When scoring use the following formula to reverse the items:

If you've circled this number on the survey: 1 2 3 4 5 6
Allocate this many points when you score: 6 5 4 3 2 1

The NP subscale contains four items all of which are reversed while subscale OP contains only one reversed item: R18. Record the number from each of the 24 items in the correct column below. Total the number of points in each column. Each column represents a dimension of critical reflection.

Your scores on each of the six critical thinking dimensions:

DI	NP	EM	OB	CA	OP
1 =	**R 2 =**	3 =	4 =	5 =	6 =
7 =	**R 8 =**	9 =	10 =	11 =	12 =
13 =	**R 14 =**	15 =	16 =	17 =	**R 18 =**
19 =	**R 20 =**	21 =	22 =	23 =	24 =
Sum =	**Sum =**	**Sum =**	**Sum =**	**Sum =**	**Sum =**

The minimum total score of all six dimensions of the CRI should be no less than 24 while the maximum should be no more than 144.

TOTAL: DI___ + NP___ + EM___ + OB___ + CA___ + OP___ =

INTERPRETING THE CRITICAL REFLECTION INVENTORY

The dimension with the lowest total is the one you perceive as being your least used skill area. The dimension with the highest total is the one you regard as being your most used skill area. A difference of more than eight points between the highest and lowest sum scores on any of the dimensions indicates a lack of flexibility in using your least regarded critical thinking ability. Scores within four points of each other indicate flexibility in using all dimensions of critical reflection. Transfer your total score on each of the six dimensions from the table above to each of the critical reflection dimensions listed on page 185.

Critical Reflection Score on DI: DIFFERENCE: _____
A high score on this dimension means that you have a high recognition of the importance of difference in your routine behavior. You actively seek different opinions and encourage others to voice their opinions, even if their values differ from your own. You are most comfortable when interacting with those who share different perspectives and you remain sensitive to different ideas.

Critical Reflection Score on NP: NON-PERSONALIZATION: _____
A high score on this dimension indicates that you feel secure about your thinking and that you are easily able to separate personal feelings from issues at hand. You normally do not become anxious if your views are challenged and rarely view such challenges as personal attacks. You seek to surface conflicting points of view, and encourage others to oppose or reject your ideas without becoming defensive.

Critical Reflection Score on EM: EMPATHY: _____
If you have a high score on this dimension, you see yourself as naturally demonstrating an appreciation of others' frames of reference. You easily appreciate what others think, what they communicate, and what they feel. You can easily detect and interpret accurately others' feelings and behaviors because you are genuinely aware of your own frame of reference.

Critical Reflection Score on OB: OBSERVATION: _____
A high score on the observation dimension of critical reflection indicates your regard for your ability to perceive and appreciate events from many points of view. You are comfortable making accurate observations of the same phenomenon from multiple perspectives while simultaneously endeavoring to improve the accuracy of your own thinking processes.

Critical Reflection Score on CA: COGNITIVE AWARENESS: _____
A high score on cognitive awareness indicates your perceived ability to understand and acknowledge your own thinking strengths and limitations, even while focusing on a problem. You tend to behave open rather than closed to ideas different from your own. You think very carefully about issues and possible solutions rather than make impulsive decisions. You probably notice others' thought processes as well as your own and are able to easily recognize when problem confusion exists.

Critical Reflection Score on OP: OPENNESS: _____
A high score on the openness dimension indicates that you feel you have the ability to identify and challenge your own assumptions. You are comfortable responding to change and improvement. You are aware of your own ideas and feelings and want to change them when you find they are not useful or worthwhile. You find it easy to change your point of view.

Consider your profile individually first and decide how accurate you really think it is. Then ask a close colleague such as your work supervisor or critical friend or partner to compete the CRI for you and score and discuss their perceptions of you versus your perceptions of yourself. The ideal result of the inventory is a balance of all six dimensions. Select which critical reflection dimensions you feel you need to develop and look back through the inventory to identify specific skills that you can practice more often so that you can develop more comfort and flexibility in using all dimensions.

HELPFUL HANDOUTS

In this section of *The 1997 McGraw-Hill Training and Performance Sourcebook,* you will find seven "helpful" handouts. These handouts cover topics such as:

✓ Communication

✓ Career planning

✓ Cross-cultural interaction

✓ Employee and management development

✓ Training methods

These handouts can be used as:

✓ Participant materials in training programs

✓ Discussion documents during meetings

✓ Coaching tools or job aids

✓ Information to be read by you or shared with a colleague

All the handouts are designed as succinct descriptions of an important issue or skill in performance management and development. They are formatted for quick, easily understood reading. (You may want to keep these handouts handy as memory joggers or checklists by posting them in your work area.) Most important of all, they contain nuggets of practical advice!

Preceding each handout is a brief overview of its contents and uses. The handout itself is on a separate page(s) to make reproduction convenient.

It is helpful to read these handouts *actively.* Highlight points that are important to you or push you to do further thinking. Identify content that needs further clarification. Challenge yourself to come up with examples that illustrate the key points. Urge others to be active consumers of these handouts, as well.

FOUR KEYS TO CROSS-CULTURAL SUCCESS

23

Donna Goldstein

Donna Goldstein, *Ed.D. is managing director of Development Associates International (3389 Sheridan St., Suite 309, Hollywood, FL 33021, 305-926-7822). She speaks, writes, and conducts training on diversity and cross-cultural issues. Donna has also taught management, human resources, and education at several South Florida universities. She is a contributor to* **20 Active Training Programs,** *vol. III (Pfeiffer, in press).*

OVERVIEW

What does it take to relate effectively to natives of countries or members of cultures other than your own? How competent are you at crossing cultures either geographically or within your organization's diverse workforce?

The Cross-Cultural Adaptability Inventory (CCAI),* first developed by Colleen Kelly and Judith Meyers in 1987, is designed to address these human resource issues. Kelly and Meyers' extensive research on cross-cultural effectiveness led them to suggest the four key components of cross-cultural success that are detailed in this handout. Combined, the components comprise the characteristics that determine an individual's cross-cultural adaptability.

Use this handout as part of a diversity training session, management briefing, or as a stand-alone article for employees to read before they venture away from their desks.

*More information on the Cross-Cultural Adaptability Inventory can be obtained from Dr. Colleen Kelly, 2500 Torrey Pines Rd., La Jolla, CA 92037 or from National Computer Systems, 800-627-7271.

FOUR KEYS TO CROSS-CULTURAL SUCCESS

Cross-cultural adaptability is essential to succeed in today's world. How do you and your employees measure up? Here are four qualities that have been found to be key to the ability to adapt to other cultures.

1. *Emotional Resilience*

Emotional resilience is the ability to "bounce back" after setbacks and difficulties. It means maintaining emotional equilibrium amid a new or changing environment. When crossing cultures, it is common to feel frustrated, confused, or alone.

Women or people of color in executive-level positions in a predominantly white-male organization will most certainly require emotional resilience if they are to learn or modify the unwritten rules and succeed. A receptionist who speaks only English and increasingly receives calls and visits from non-English speakers also requires emotional resilience.

If the workforce and marketplace continue to diversify as predicted, staff at every level will have to learn to adjust to new situations and develop the skills to deal with the complexities of cross-cultural situations.

2. *Flexibility and Openness*

Flexibility and openness suggest a tolerance for ambiguity and an openness to new experiences. When living or working within other cultures, people frequently encounter ideas or behavior different from their own. A flexible and open person respects and tries to explore cultural differences, refusing to succumb to prejudice or bias. Such a person also moves beyond ethnocentrism to accept alternatives to "the way we've always done things" at a particular company or country.

The "ugly American" stereotype may well have stemmed from a lack of development in this dimension, as demonstrated by both U.S. tourists and businesspeople abroad. Flexibility and openness are required to maintain a workforce that is able to think creatively, take risks, and draw from the wisdom of all peoples and cultures.

3. Perceptual Acuity

Other cultures' unfamiliar or confusing expressions, assumptions, body language, customs, or values can make communication difficult. High perceptual acuity means demonstrating empathy and understanding both verbal and nonverbal cues in the environment.

Many conflicts between African-Americans and Anglos stem from misperceptions on both sides regarding such cues as voice tone and demonstrated respect. Several incidents have demonstrated how an Asian man's modesty, which is esteemed in his culture, could be mistaken for a lack of competence or assertiveness in the United States. With both clients and coworkers, perceptual acuity is essential to prevent misunderstandings and encourage clear communication.

4. Personal Autonomy

Personal autonomy means having a strong sense of awareness and acceptance of one's self as a valuable and unique individual. In a new environment, people may not receive the reactions and reinforcement to which they are accustomed. As organizations become more automated and personal, staff members must feel a sense of self-worth and respect for their individuality to work cohesively.

As employees of all backgrounds work in other regions or countries, this challenge increases. A native Nicaraguan born to British and West Indian parents may feel uncomfortable filling out forms that give him choices such as "black," "white," or "Hispanic." However, mixed heritage often causes more concern to others than it does to the individual himself.

When interacting with those who have different ethnic or racial backgrounds, gender, age, or sexual preferences, one's own sense of self can be put to the test; yet it must remain strong for an individual to succeed.

PRACTICAL POINTERS FOR PERSUASIVE MEMOS

24

Juliet Musso

Juliet Musso, *Ph.D. is an Assistant Professor in Public Policy (School of Public Administration, University of Southern California, Los Angeles, CA 90089, 213-740-0001 musso@usc.edu). She has research and teaching expertise in federalism, intergovernmental management, urban political economy, and microeconomic policy analysis. Her specific research interests include intergovernmental finance, fiscal federalism reform, and the effects of alternative governance structures on agenda setting and political voice and exit.*

OVERVIEW

Need to create a memo that has impact? One that really draws in readers and encourages them to keep on reading until the end? Here is a handout that identifies both general and specific ways to create memos that persuade. The writing tips come from the author's experiences in the public sector and discussions with public managers and policy analysts.

PRACTICAL POINTERS FOR PERSUASIVE MEMOS

The ability to persuade is essential to public policy and management, and the memorandum is a common vehicle for persuasion. In general, persuasive memos have three major characteristics: They are decisive, compelling, and brief.

Decisiveness is crucial because nobody appreciates a manager who wavers. Try to avoid double-handed discussion ("on the one hand, but then on the other") and empty recommendations ("we need to study this further ..."). When you truly cannot make a decision and must defer to someone higher in the organization, make the issues involved very clear and identify the tradeoffs or risks facing the decision maker.

The degree to which your memo is ***compelling*** depends heavily on its analytic quality. Frame the issue appropriately, reason it through, and support your reasoning with convincing facts and examples. Solid logic backed by evidence is compelling to the reader. Although form should not dominate content, you can *enhance* your memo's content through skillful presentation.

Brevity is the third characteristic of a memo that has impact. Your reader must be able to understand the memo's message in *two minutes or less*. If readers cannot immediately understand your main point within this time period they will be unlikely to read further.

More specifically, persuasive memos are well-structured and well-written. Here are some practical pointers to help your memos persuade others to your point of view.

1. **Start with the bottom line.** The memo should begin with a very brief summary of the major issue and your conclusions or recommendations. What is the most important point to get across? Your conclusion. So get to it! You want to ensure that your reader understands the bottom line after a thirty-second reading.

2. **End with a bang.** Cognitive psychologists have found that people remember information best from the beginning and the end of a sequence. If you put your bottom line first, you should either restate it or place your most compelling evidence at the end of the memo. Similarly, if you are listing key points, put the least important material in the middle of the list.

3. **Keep it simple and straightforward.** Your memo should be readily comprehensible to someone who does not know or care about your organization and its problems. Also known as the "New York Taxi Driver Test," a straightforward memo uses plain language, avoids bureaucratic or social science jargon, and keeps technical background in footnotes or appendices. Even if you base your conclusions on a complicated linear programming model, you nonetheless should be able to explain your reasoning to your cab driver.

4. **Present information selectively.** A common pitfall is to snow the reader with gratuitous supporting evidence. If one or two reasons are persuasive, let them stand alone. Your other arguments are valuable reserve ammunition. You may agonize over the right recommendation, but your reader should come away thinking that your conclusions are so strong as to be virtually self-evident.

5. **Anticipate objections.** This is not to say that you should ignore weaknesses in the analysis. You should always anticipate arguments from the opposition. In some cases, you will want to acknowledge and refute an opposing viewpoint within the memo. Elsewhere it makes more sense to ignore counter-arguments and marshal responding evidence for a subsequent memo or presentation. This is a strategic question that you will have to address within the context of the specific issue.

6. **Be creative in your presentation.** Set key sections of the memo off with informative and catchy headings. Use bullet points, italics, or bold face to highlight key points. Avoid massive paragraphs and leave a lot of white space.

7. **Include visual aids where appropriate.** Creative graphs and tables can catch the reader's attention, but don't go overboard. The point of the graph or table should be evident at a glance, and its title should state the point (e.g., Figure 1: Budget deficit will grow fifteen percent over three years).

8. **Know your audience.** If your agency head is a numbers jockey who loves technical detail, by all means include it. Some audiences respond to a humorous tone, while others prefer a dry and detached approach.

9. **Proofread your work.** And then proofread it again. Remember to double-check that your tables sum up properly. Although such details may seem petty, minor errors can undermine the credibility of the most brilliant analysis.

If proofreading is not your forte, here are several strategies that will be helpful to you: (1) use a ruler to proof each line separately; (2) proof once from top to bottom, then reverse and proof bottom to top; and (3) on monumentally important memos, ask an associate to double-check your work. If you include personal names, be *absolutely certain* that you spell them correctly.

10. **Strunk and White.** If you don't have it, get it. Two other thought-provoking pieces on writing are:

George Orwell. (1984) "Politics and the English Language," reprinted in *The Orwell Reader: Fiction, Essays and Reportage.* Harcourt Brace Jovanovich.

Annie Lamott. (1994) *Bird by Bird: Some Instructions on Writing and Life.* New York: Pantheon Books.

THE TEN FR**25**EDOMS OF EMPOWERMENT

Cynthia Solomon

Cynthia Solomon, *Ph.D. is a technical program specialist for FERMCO, an environmental restoration company in Ohio (6469 Fountains Blvd., West Chester, OH 45069, 513-777-5435). Cindy has led or designed organizational and professional development projects for her employer, the health care industry, and professional and private organizations. She authored* **TQM in Dietetics and Nutrition Services,** *and has designed several training and management documents. She also manages a private human resources development practice. Cynthia was a contributor to* **The 1996 McGraw-Hill Team and Organization Development Sourcebook.**

OVERVIEW

When we speak of empowering employees, we speak about giving them the responsibility to perform their work and the required level of authority to plan that work and make decisions. Managers who empower their employees have to give up a little of their own power and authority to the employee. Take some time to review *The Ten Freedoms of Empowerment* with your employees to insure that you are reaping the full benefits of an empowered workforce.

THE TEN FREEDOMS OF EMPOWERMENT

Empowerment offers employees the freedom to:

1. Propose and Develop New Ideas

Some, if not most, of the best ideas for developing new and better products and services for our customers come from our employees. An empowered employee knows that his ideas are welcomed and valued at any stage of development. His willingness to come forward with new ideas is rewarded, even if the idea cannot be accepted.

2. Disagree without Being Considered a Disagreeable Person

Having someone with a different perspective feel free to offer her points of disagreement may be the way a company identifies problems before customers do! What would be worse—an employee who disagreed about some aspect of work, or an employee who found a problem with work, but said nothing because she feared reprisal? How to disagree in a constructive manner is a useful skill and can be coached.

3. Have His Alternative Ideas Fairly Considered

A work culture that empowers its employees acknowledges that some of them may have a "better way to build the mouse trap." Decisions are not made in an empowered work culture without considering viable alternatives.

4. Make a Mistake

Show me a company where no one makes mistakes, and I'll show you a company where no one works! Mistakes show us how not to do things, which in turn gives us insight into better options. An empowered workforce not only acknowledges that it makes mistakes, it finds ways to share both mistakes and lessons learned so that others will not repeat the same mistake.

5. Be Spared from Embarrassment (Particularly in the Presence of Others)

There is no excuse for any manager to embarrass any employee at any time. There are constructive ways to correct unacceptable work performance.

6. Receive a Fair Performance Appraisal

An empowered employee is given a fair performance appraisal, using criteria that are made known to her at the beginning of work and applied consistently in the same manner as with other employees. A fair performance appraisal is preceded by manager-directed discussions and counseling/-coaching when ineffective work is observed. A fair performance appraisal is not a surprise report of problems.

7. Establish Necessary Lines of Communication to Accomplish Work

An empowered employee is not encumbered by a steep organizational hierarchy as he attempts to establish necessary lines of communication in order to perform his work. He should be allowed to call those he needs to call. Imagine how silly is the situation in which Joe must call Jane's secretary to get permission to have a meeting with Jim to brief him on a project that he is doing for Kathy!

8. Establish Her Own Work Schedule and Work Approach

An empowered employee is the manager of her own work. Her manager should be interested in the results of that work, and less interested in the details of the process. Work schedules and approaches are developed by the empowered employee and presented to the manager for approval.

9. Expect Constructive Feedback

Empowered employees know that feedback throughout a work process helps identify quality issues and solve them before they have a serious effect on the quality of the finished product. An empowered employee knows that he may seek feedback from those whose opinion he wants or needs, and that feedback will be constructive.

10. Present Credentials for Promotions or Other Assignments within the Company

Empowered employees feel welcomed to present themselves fairly for other employment opportunities (lateral and horizontal moves), and know that their credentials will be considered fairly. The power to seek advancement is theirs.

26
SEVEN TRAINING PITFALLS AND WHAT YOU CAN DO TO OVERCOME THEM

Kevin Eikenberry

Kevin Eikenberry *is president of the Discian Group (7035 Bluffridge Way, Indianapolis, IN 46278, 317-387-1424, kevin@discian.com, http://www.performancepartners.com), a consulting firm focusing on organizational learning, training trainers, instructional design, team building, and leading change. Kevin is a member of the American Society for Training and Development and the International Society for Performance Improvement, and is chair of the board of directors of the North American Simulation and Gaming Association. He is also a contributor to* **20 Active Training Programs,** *vol. III (Pfeiffer, in press) and* **The 1996 McGraw-Hill Training and Performance Sourcebook.**

OVERVIEW

Abraham Maslow said "If the only tool you have is a hammer, every problem looks like a nail." Managers, leaders, and change agents all want to improve organizational performance. Training is often seen as our major tool in this pursuit. While training can be a fabulous tool for providing awareness, knowledge, and skills, it sometimes fails to achieve the desired results. Why? This handout identifies the seven most common training pitfalls, and gives you specific action steps to take to avoid these problems in the future.

SEVEN TRAINING PITFALLS

1. The "Who's Accountable?" Game

Participants rarely are held accountable for using what they learned in a course or workshop when they get back to the workplace. Consequently, participants recognize going to training as a game. That's why training is seldom seen (by anyone in the organization) as what it should be—a strategic part of the business, with responsibility for performance enhancement. Regardless of how training is viewed, if participants aren't held accountable, how likely is it that real performance change will occur? All of the actions below will make accountability clear.

What You Can Do:

✓ Give participants a clear message before going to training what the expectations will be for them when they return.

✓ Plan to spend some time with the participants both before and after the training session to preview and review learning.

✓ Let participants know before they attend training that an action plan is expected as a result of the session. (Then be interested in the outcome.)

✓ Ask participants how you can help them reach their new performance goals.

2. The Cafeteria Cause—"Course du Jour"

Often training has no connection to the strategic objectives of the organization. Whether true or not, the prevalent perception in the organization is that there is no rhyme or reason to the latest training course. This common pitfall is called "Course du Jour" because new training is offered as often as some people try new diets. With popular diets, people hear about the new approach, buy the book, get excited, try the new tricks, and soon leave it—usually before they receive any real benefit. The same thing happens in an organization. There's usually nothing wrong with the training introduced, except that it lacks organizational support and the time to work. In these instances, the company is wasting effort, confusing the majority of the employees, and perhaps most costly, building cynicism and reducing the credibility of the leadership.

What You Can Do:

✓ Make training decisions based on strategic direction and real performance gaps. Once those training priorities have been set, stick to them.

✓ Make a commitment to get a return on that training investment.

✓ Resolve to give the training time and support to work.

✓ Determine clear performance outcomes for the effort *up front.*

✓ Ask yourself, "How does this fit with what we've been doing? Is this just our next 'diet'?"

✓ Integrate real work into the training when possible.

3. *The Piling on the Work Paradigm*

Managers and leaders often see training as an expensive waste of time. When they attend classes, they obsess about all the work that is piling up "back in the office." Their employees see this attitude through their leader's actions. This disease grows in "the ranks" because leaders don't explain the reasons for the course and don't help them deal with the workload while they are gone. Since you can't "make" participants learn, these situations can be disastrous in the training session itself. Participants may resent having to be in training because they don't understand why they're there, and they know they'll have to work harder when they get back to the job to catch up. In this situation, the participants may leave more cynical than when they arrived, with few if any new skills to counteract that possible effect.

What You Can Do:

✓ Do everything possible to make sure *all* of management is on-board with the training and its purpose.

✓ Make a commitment to get a return on that training investment.

✓ Resolve to give training the time and support to work.

✓ Determine clear performance outcomes for the effort *up front.*

✓ Set up a plan to handle work while the participant is learning. This action speaks volumes about the importance of the training. It will also improve their ability to focus on the session (e.g. "My critical work is being handled," and "Whew, I'm sure glad that most of my mail will have been opened when I get back!").

4. *The January Third Application Assignment*

Well-designed training with motivated learners will result in participants leaving the session with some clear ideas about how they plan to apply what they've learned back on the job. But well-intentioned as those plans might be, they may be no more

effective than most New Year's Resolutions. Old habits are hard to break! Habits are especially hard to break when there is no support for new skills and behaviors back in the workplace.

What You Can Do:

✓ Give participants a clear message before going to training what the expectations will be for them when they return.

✓ Let them know before they attend a session that an action plan is expected as a result of the training. (Then be interested in the outcome.)

✓ Ask participants how you can help them reach their new performance goals.

✓ Give an entire work group training in new information and skills at the same time (whenever possible and appropriate).

✓ Integrate real work into training when possible.

5. The Sleepwear Syndrome—"One-Size-Fits-All"

T-shirts or sleepwear are often sold with tags that read "one-size-fits-all." Training isn't sleepwear and is not as effective if sold in a similar manner. Too often, generic, across-the-board training becomes the norm in an organization. The basic premise with this syndrome is that "We'll give it to everyone as a way of being fair. If not everyone needs this information or lacks the skills, we will at least make sure that we haven't left anyone out." The reality behind one-size-fits-all training is that it is used when management doesn't really know what specific new skills are necessary for their various employees.

What You Can Do:

✓ Base training and attendance decisions on specific skills that are needed to be effective in the workplace.

6. The Lone Ranger Situation

Participants are sometimes sent to training as a perk, a reward, or as a way to get them into a new environment for awhile. In most cases, people in a team or work group may never all receive the same training, except for the "Course du Jour" or "One-Size-Fits-All" variety. Sometimes people need specific skills to perform a specific part of their work. Often though, the "perk" training offered is for skills many people in the group could use (or maybe they'll be sent over time; after all, everyone can't be gone at once). The result? Participants come back to work in a vacuum. Not only are they not accountable (see pitfall #1), but no one

they work with has the same new skills and knowledge that they do. Without support, the new ideas a Lone Ranger brings back may not get implemented due to peer resistance or ignorance.

What You Can Do:

✓ Give an entire work group training in new information and skills at the same time (whenever possible and appropriate).

✓ Build training that is linked to the problems at work.

✓ Integrate real work into the training when possible.

7. The "Name That Tune" Show

This problem arises when, in the name of expediency or efficiency, training time is compacted. Trainers are asked to "Name That Tune" (or complete the training) in shorter and shorter time blocks. This show starts with "The Management Team only needs an overview," and ends with training being designed to fit a time slot, as opposed to being designed to build specific skills. The typical result of the "Name That Tune—shorten the session for my people" Game is training that is little more than *exposure* to a topic area, not training that can transfer real skills, with real practice time in the classroom.

What You Can Do:

✓ Give the training staff some muscle—let them push back hard for training that is skill-based, and not just meant to fill an ever-shortening time slot.

✓ Determine clear performance outcomes for the effort *up front.*

FIFTEEN PRACTICAL WAYS TO IMPROVE COMPUTER TRAINING

27

Shirley Copeland

Shirley Copeland, *Ed.D. is an education and training consultant (6018 Bitternut Drive, Alexandria, VA 22310, 703-971-3381). She specializes in instructional design, curriculum development, and performance analysis. Her research focuses on employee orientation and evaluation of training.*

OVERVIEW

Computer training is a challenging job that requires an understanding of learning and instruction principles as well as knowledge of a particular system or software program. Computer trainers are usually well-versed in the technicalities of their subject matter, but may exhibit weaknesses in their knowledge of instructional design and delivery principles. This handout provides some basic tips for improving computer-related skills instruction.

FIFTEEN WAYS TO IMPROVE COMPUTER TRAINING

1. *Demonstrate* how to use a system's keys or functions as you talk about them. This process helps the learner to begin forming mental models, i.e., conceptual representations of how the system or a feature works. Mental models aid in memory retention and learning transfer.

2. *Chunk* information in small pieces to make it easier for the learner to retain. Cognitive psychologists have determined that the most pieces of information that individuals can retain in their short-term memory is between five and seven informational or idea units.

3. *Link* new information with previously learned information. It's important to continually emphasize how functions, keys, and processes are interrelated to provide learning reinforcement.

4. *Relate* elements of instruction to specific job tasks. For instance, when explaining a concept such as "find and replace," don't talk about the concept in terms of looking for one word and replacing it with another. Instead, discuss the concept in terms of a problem situation that learners will likely encounter in their daily use. Encourage participants to think of ways they would be able to use a particular process or function in performing their job duties and tasks.

5. *Guide* learners through practice activities to help them clarify processes that were misunderstood and to apply their newly learned skills in a safe, nonthreatening environment.

6. *Design* exercises to build on previously learned functions and keys. The more opportunities that the learner has to apply the concepts and functions, the greater the likelihood of transfer to the job.

7. *Associate* concepts or processes with familiar events or contexts to help learners to integrate the information better. Use analogies to explain certain concepts or try other creative approaches to convey complex information in easily understandable terms.

8. *Summarize* often to help learners focus on what has occurred and to help them relate what they have learned to existing knowledge.

9. *Use* materials, examples, exercises, and activities that are relevant to the learner to make learning more meaningful.

10. *Diagnose* learner errors to help learners figure out what they did wrong. Encourage discussions about how to correct an error.

11. *Challenge* and *motivate* learners with a variety of exercises and activities.

12. *Encourage* collaboration with others through team activities or group learning projects.

13. *Vary* the instructional sequencing for more robust learning. For instance, if you're dealing with a complex function, break it down in sequential steps to enable the learner to master each step before proceeding to the next level. For simpler tasks, provide a general overview instead of a detailed procedural approach.

14. *Respect* the learner. Avoid using denigrating remarks and provide constructive feedback.

15. *Listen* to the learners' questions and empathize with them.

FOUR STEP**28**TO CAREER SUCCESS

Michaeline Skiba

Michaeline (Mickey) Skiba *(Tall Oaks Apts., Pavilion Rd. #3, Suffern, NY 10901, 914-369-6217) is a senior education specialist for Novadigm, Inc. and doctoral candidate in the Communications, Computing & Technology Department of Columbia University. She is a contributor to* **20 Active Training Programs,** *vol. III (Pfeiffer, in press). Mickey was also a contributor to* **The 1996 McGraw-Hill Training and Performance Sourcebook.**

OVERVIEW

The meaning of the word "career" continues to change. Some experts believe that the era of the lifelong job with one company has disappeared, while others think job-hopping is merely another fad that will diminish over time. Regardless of these or your own attitudes about work, one thing has been and always will be certain: Each of us is responsible for our own career.

The following tips were gathered from colleagues, bosses, friends, and personal experiences in the marketplace. Since career planning is more of an art than a science, these tips emphasize the interpersonal/relational dimensions of the process rather than the mechanical steps so frequently found in "how to" books or outplacement firms. Use these ideas throughout all the stages of your life to help your career goals stay on track.

FOUR STEPS TO CAREER SUCCESS

1. Preparation: Research

For the young professional:

✓ Cast a wide net. You haven't narrowed your work life to one industry or profession yet, so you're not "pigeonholed." Examine all of your career possibilities by using directories such as *Moody's, Dun & Bradstreet,* and *Standard & Poors* to broaden your options.

✓ Don't worry about having "enough" experience. Apply your strengths to what you've done, and seek out chances to do more and to learn more. Write a resume that emphasizes how you've performed for part-time employers, school-related clubs, and civic and community organizations.

For the seasoned professional:

✓ Forget the rules—there aren't any anymore! Industry-hopping is a common practice. Think globally if you can.

✓ Get connected electronically. The Internet is easy to use, fun, and a valuable tool for finding small to mid-sized firms that offer unique opportunities.

✓ Don't stop learning. Although experience and formal education are both valuable commodities, current, relevant information is priceless. Take a course or class to reactivate yourself. The "knowledge worker" is here to stay.

2. Action: Being Visible

✓ No one ever hired a resume. Networking means getting in front of people who can help you. If you're shy, you'll need to work on this one.

✓ Help people. Make yourself memorable by being in the right place at the right time. Proactivity counts. Besides, it feels good to lend a hand.

✓ Make presentations wherever you can. They add to your visibility and help sharpen your interviewing skills.

3. Reaction: Making the Right Choices

✓ Don't cave in to foolish offers. Just because the job market may be temporarily weak, you don't have to roll over and play dead. Be realistic yet fair to yourself.

✓ Create your "ideal scene." Visualize what you've always wanted to do or be, and start creating it. Athletes and salespeople frequently use this mental technique to overcome the competition—why don't you?

✓ Everything is temporary. View your career/jobs as only one dimension of your total self. Don't fall into the trap of believing that a job is like a death. Unlike any job, a death is permanent. Reprioritize when necessary.

4. Continuation: The Search Never Ends

✓ Keep in touch with people who have helped you. Send them holiday cards or news articles that would interest them. Stay continuously visible.

✓ Keep in touch with people whom you like as people. Regardless of the challenges surrounding a job search, maintain your humanity.

✓ Above all else, do what you love. You'll be happy, you'll be motivated, and the chances are in your favor that you'll be good at it.

A CHECKLIST FOR WRITING QUALITY PRINT MATERIAL

Kavita Gupta

Kavita Gupta *is an independent consultant specializing in assessment and training systems design (Targeted Training, 28 Pilgrim Drive, Winchester, MA 01890, 617-721-6440). Kavita previously developed and managed training programs for Citicorp and a major performance improvement consulting company. She has been published in national ASTD & ISPI publications, spoken at conferences, and served on the boards of several ASTD chapters.*

OVERVIEW

The use of print material in the workplace has increased significantly in the past decade. Administrative, professional, technical, and managerial jobs require enhanced skills in digesting and reacting to information quickly. How much is learned or retained depends on how effectively the message is presented. Whether you are developing a simple marketing brochure, guidebook, or other piece of print material, it is important that your document is professional and delivers results.

An important consideration prior to developing any document is an understanding of your audience. The document should be tailored to the educational background and readability level of your end user. A document written at the eighth-grade level is appropriate for shop floor employees with high school educations. On the other hand, a writing style comparable to the Wall Street Journal might be used for a document targeted at an audience with graduate or postgraduate degrees.

The following handout is useful to anyone who develops or oversees the development of print material. This easy to use checklist provides a step-by-step guide that can be followed to ensure that a document meets the highest quality standards. Key questions relate to the motivational appeal, structure and organization, clarity, presentation, layout and design of the document, and use of graphics. Use the checklist the next time you want to create print material that really gets its message across.

PRINT MATERIAL CHECKLIST

✓ *Motivational Appeal*

❑ Is there an eye-catching phrase, quote, or visual on the cover to grab the reader's initial attention?

❑ Is the document visually appealing to the reader?

❑ Does the document reflect the culture and tone of the audience or organization for which it is being designed? (For example, a brochure using primary colors could be used for salespeople, but earth tones might be more appropriate in a corporate or business setting.)

✓ *Structure and Organization*

❑ Does a brief introduction tell the reader about the who, what, why, when, and how of the document?

❑ Are explanations for any special design features included?

❑ Are ideas grouped under clearly delineated headings and subheadings?

❑ Do ideas logically follow a top-down or bottom-up approach?

❑ Is backward or forward chaining used when transitioning between groups of ideas to maintain continuity and flow?

❑ For documents with long sections, are brief summaries included before a new idea is presented?

✓ *Clarity*

❑ Are sentences limited to 12 to 17 words?

❑ Are sentences joined by ifs or ands used only when necessary?

❑ Is active voice used instead of passive voice?

❑ Have redundant words been eliminated?

❑ Is there information overload (e.g., too many concepts or ideas in one paragraph)?

- ❑ Are new concepts supported by examples, illustrations, or brief explanations?

- ❑ Have difficult words been replaced with simpler words (e.g., use prove instead of substantiate)?

- ❑ Have technical words or jargon been eliminated or simplified?

- ❑ Do checklists use simple and consistent language?

- ❑ Are checklists organized into groups of tasks or actions?

- ❑ If checklists are used to document completion of steps, are actions written in the order in which they should be performed?

- ❑ Are checklists free of negatives?

✓ *Presentation*

- ❑ Can headings be presented in the form of questions?

- ❑ Do advanced organizers prepare the audience for what they will be reading?

- ❑ Can key concepts or ideas be replaced with diagrams or pictorials?

- ❑ Are pie charts, graphs, or tables supported by keys or legends?

- ❑ Do explanations or summaries immediately precede or follow graphical illustrations?

- ❑ Are lists of actions grouped into bullet points?

- ❑ Are instructions clear and concise?

✓ *Layout and Design*

- ❑ Is there consistency in format, type style, or typeface throughout the document?

- ❑ Is there variety in typeface and type style to draw the reader's attention to key concepts or ideas?

- ❑ Is text readable? (8- to 10-point type is difficult to read.)

- ❑ Are ragged or unjustified margins used?

- ❏ Are both lower case and upper case used instead of all caps?

- ❏ Is there balance between text, bullet points, and white space?

✓ *Graphics*

- ❏ Are graphics relevant and appropriate for the audience or industry?

- ❏ Are graphics of high quality and resolution?

- ❏ Are graphics gender appropriate and bias-free?

- ❏ Are pictures or drawings proportionate to real-life objects or characters?

- ❏ Are line drawings instead of pictures used to show complex items such as equipment or machinery?

- ❏ Are all graphics clearly labeled, numbered, or referenced to relevant text?

- ❏ Do color schemes complement each other?

- ❏ Do flowcharts use small steps?

- ❏ Do flowcharts present only one choice at each decision point?

- ❏ Are flowchart decisions presented in descending order from more important to less important?

- ❏ If a series of flowcharts is presented, are they labeled to show continuity or connected by arrows?

PRACTICAL GUIDES

In this section of *The 1997 McGraw-Hill Training and Performance Sourcebook,* you will find eleven practical guides. These "how to" guides are short articles containing useful ideas and guidelines for implementing training and performance support initiatives.

You will find advice about such topics as:

✓ Coaching, supervising, and mentoring

✓ Evaluation of training

✓ Development of training materials

✓ Learning and performance alternatives

✓ Employee development

Each guide contains step-by-step advice. Several have examples, illustrations, charts, and tables to enhance your understanding of the content. You will find that these guides are clearly organized and easy to read.

Four suggested uses for the practical guides are:

1. Guidelines for your own consulting, facilitating, and training interventions.
2. Implementation advice to be shared with peers and people who report to you.
3. Recommendations to senior management.
4. Reading assignments in training programs.

HOW TO GIVE GREAT ADVICE AND FEEDBACK

30

Chip Bell

Chip R. Bell *is a senior partner with Performance Research Associates, Inc. and manages their Dallas, TX office (25 Highland Park #100, Dallas, TX 75205, 214-522-5777, prawest@aol.com). He is the author of ten books, including* **Customers As Partners** *and* **Managing Knock Your Socks Off Service.** *This article is adapted from his newest book* Managers as Mentors: Building Partnerships for Learning (*San Francisco: Berrett-Koehler Publishers, 1996).*

Here is a first-person account of how to handle the often difficult process of giving advice and feedback. Although this guide is oriented specifically toward mentors and their protégés, the same information can easily be applied to a variety of management situations.

Someone once asked famed Notre Dame head football coach Lou Holtz what he considered to be the toughest part of his job. With his typical "aw shucks" charm he finessed the question, but ultimately communicated that one of the hardest parts was "teaching lessons that stay taught." Mentors have a similar challenge.

Mentoring actions can range from chalkboard-side teaching to a spirited discussion to circulation of relevant articles. But one of the most challenging parts of mentoring is the giving of advice and feedback. Recall the last time someone said, "Let me give you a little advice … or feedback!" No doubt it quickly put you in a defensive posture. Psychologists remind us that we all have "authority hangups" of varying degrees. Your protégé does as well! And, protégé resistance to and resentment of mentor advice and feedback creates the challenge in "teaching lessons that stay taught." As one frustrated supervisor commented, "I tell 'em what they ought to do, but it seems to go in one ear and out the other!"

Giving Advice Without Getting Resistance

Advice giving works only if the context is learning—that is, when you are offering advice because you believe the output of the protégé will be improved if knowledge or skill is enhanced. The reason this is important is that for advice giving to truly work you must be ready for the protégé to *not* take your advice. If the protégé has no real choice as to whether or not to honor your advice, then you should simply give a directive and be done with it. Couching your requirement as advice is manipulative, and will only foster distrust and resentment.

Below are four steps that can make giving advice more powerful *and* more productive. The steps are numbered, implying that the sequence is crucial to success.

Step 1. Clearly State the Performance Problem or Goal

Begin giving advice by letting the protégé know the focus or intent of your mentoring. You may be offering advice regarding improvement of performance. It might be a new skill the protégé is trying to master. And, it sounds like this: "Pat, I wanted to talk with you about the fact that your last quarter call rate was up, but your sales were down 20%." For advice to work it is vital you be very specific and clear in your statement. Ambiguity clouds the conversation and risks leaving the protégé more confused than assisted.

Stating the focus helps sort out several dimensions. Is the performance problem or goal related to something not working or broken or something needing to be added? Stated differently, is the objective of the advice related to a skill deficiency (requiring mentoring) or will deficiency (requiring coaching)? Being clear up front about the focal point of your advice leads you away from scattergun thoughts toward laser-like advice.

Step 2. Make Sure You Agree on the Focus

If what you see as a performance challenge is seen by the protégé as otherwise, your advice will be viewed as overcontrolling or smothering. Make sure the protégé is as anxious to improve or learn as you are to see him or her improve or learn. You may discover that the protégé has already determined what to do and has little need for your advice. Your goal is to hear the protégé say something like: "Yes, I have been concerned about that as well."

What do you do if you determine something the protégé needs to learn and the protégé either disagrees learning is needed or is unwilling to learn what you want to teach? Many lessons get "taught" (not learned) under this scenario! As Abraham Lincoln said, "A person convinced against his will is of the same opinion still."

Take a broader perspective. If performance is a factor, be sure to have objective information (as a tool, not as proof) that is helpful in collectively examining needs. If all else fails, delay the conversation to a time when the protégé demonstrates a greater readiness to learn. To abuse the old adage, "You can lead a horse to water, but you cannot make him think!" While protégé are by no means horses, they can sometimes be as stubborn. Never resist resistance!

Step 3. Ask Permission to Give Advice

This is the most important step! Your goal at this point is twofold: 1) to communicate advice without surfacing protégé resistance, and 2) to leave ownership of the challenge with the protégé. This does not mean saying, "May I have your permission to ...?" It does mean saying something like, "I have some ideas on how you might improve if that would be helpful to you." I know what you're thinking. What fool is going to admit they are not interested in the boss' advice? Remember, the goal is to communicate in a way that minimizes the protégé being controlled or coerced, or feeling controlled.

The essence of resistance is control. None of us is enthused about being told what to do; some are more insurgent than others. What happens if, despite your best efforts, you sense protégé resistance? Again, the first rule is to never resist resistance. Back off! Take a second to examine your stance, tone, and choice of words to ascertain if you might be inadvertently fueling the resistance.

Name the issue and take the hit! Sometimes, simply surfacing your perception in a low-key, understated way and assuming you are the culprit can pull the tension from the situation. It might sound something like: "I could be wrong on this, but I worry that I may have come on too strong just now and implied that I was commanding you. That was not my intent."

Step 4. State Your Advice in the First Person Singular

Phrases like "you ought to" quickly raise listener resistance! Keeping your advice in the first person singular—"what *I* found helpful" or "what worked for *me*"—helps eliminate the "shoulds" and "ought tos." The protégé will hear such advice without the internal noise of defensiveness or resistance. Advice that goes unheard goes unheeded.

A major part of mentoring is the giving of advice. Advice can be like a game of pinball. Only by pushing and pulling can you encourage the ball to go in a new direction, increasing the score. But too much pushing and pulling can cause the pinball machine to register "tilt," and the game is over. Effective mentors recognize the challenge of "teaching so it stays taught." They meet that challenge by coupling their wisdom with sensitivity.

Giving Feedback Without Getting Resentment

What's the difference between giving feedback and giving advice? We could create an artificial distinction, a made-up definition that sounds wise and profound. However, let's just say at the outset that the concepts are similar. But there is one key difference that makes giving feedback more challenging than giving advice. First, some background.

In the late 1960's I worked in Vietnam as an Army infantry unit commander. Attached to my combat unit was an artillery officer who worked as the forward observer (FO) for the artillery unit in the rear that supported our field operations. This FO essentially served as the "eyes" for the gunner pulling the "lanyard" on the artillery piece ("cannon"). As rounds (very big bullets) were fired several miles out, the FO observed their impact, and, using a field radio, called in the corrections, all aimed at improving the accuracy of the next shot. The FO never made "Lousy shot" or "Well, that was better than last week" commentaries on their accuracy. He simply called back "Drop 100 meters" as a correction or "Pay dirt" as a confirmation. The FO had a perspective the gunner needed and did not have.

Advice is about adding information; feedback is fundamentally about filling a blind spot. There is, however, a key difference between artillery feedback and mentoring feedback. Artillery feedback is not likely to unearth recipient wrath. And, the "blindness" factor makes protégé feedback a tricky gift! How does a mentor bestow a gift that by its basic nature reminds the protégé of his or her inability to see it? How do you fill a perceptual gap and have the recipient focus on the gift, not the gap, to focus on the filled side of a half-filled hole?

"But, what about confirming feedback?" you may be thinking. "Surely protégés won't resent feedback that provides confirmation that their efforts were 'on target'!"

Be careful! There is great potential that well-intentioned confirmation can be heard by the protégé as patronizing or unnecessary. Your confirming, "This report you wrote was complete and effective" can provoke in the mind of a protégé a caustic "What gives you the right to tell me this?"

For several years I had an acquaintance who was legally blind (today we would call her visually challenged). She was not self-conscious about her malady. At a dinner party she was asked by a close friend, "What is the hardest part about being blind?" Her answer: "When people assist me, I sometimes cannot tell if the help I am being given is for my preservation or their pretension." The giving of confirming feedback should contain the same level of care as the giving of corrective feedback.

Advice is expertise the protégé may have or could acquire. Our hostile "Keep your advice to yourself" or "I don't need your darn advice" is as much about timing as relevance. The potential resistance is therefore about "premature smartness," that is, "You (the mentor) are telling me (the protégé) something you have which, in time, I might/will acquire on my own." But, with feedback the issue is one of "You (the mentor) are telling me something you have which (given your perspective) I will never acquire on my own (and that makes me irritated)." As the issue with advice is potential resistance, the issue with feedback is potential resentment.

Below are four steps that can make the giving of feedback more powerful *and* more productive. The steps are numbered, and again, the order is vital to effectiveness.

Step 1. Create a Climate of Identification ("I'm Like You")

A key factor of the blind spot component of feedback is the protégé's embarrassment over the spot. Granted, "embarrassment" might at times be too strong a label for the protégé's feelings; it is at other times not strong enough. Nonetheless, the mentor's goal is to assist the protégé's receptivity for feedback by creating a climate of identification. Seek comments that have an "I'm like you, that is, not perfect or flawless" kind of message. This need not be a major production or overdone. Just a sentence or two can establish rapport.

Step 2. State the Rationale for Feedback

Because of the lack of perspective caused by the blind spot, the protégé will need a context to hear the feedback. This is not a plea for subtlety or diplomacy as much as a petition for creating a readiness for gap filling. Help the protégé gain a clear sense of why the feedback is being given. Ensure there is a perspective that facilitates the making sense side of the feedback. Assume you want to give feedback and never leave the protégé wondering "Why is he/she telling me this? or "How in the world can I benefit from this feedback?"

Step 3. Assume You Are Giving You the Feedback

That feedback should be laced with clarity and empathy is obvious. We know that we more accurately hear feedback that is delivered in a sensitive and unambiguous fashion. However, there is another key dimension to the effective giving of feedback. It should possess the utmost integrity. This means it is straight and honest. Frankness is not about cruelty; it is about insuring the receiver does not walk away wondering, "What did he or she *not* tell me, that I needed to hear?" Trust is born out of clean communication. Think of your goal this way: How would you deliver the feedback if you were giving *you* the feedback? Take your cue from your own preferences.

Step 4. Ask for What You Gave—Feedback

The interpersonal ground on which you both stand is made more reliable by your solicitation of feedback on your delivery. Not only is this useful to you for the future, it telegraphs the leveling playing field of the partnership. The forward observer attached to my 82nd Airborne unit from time to time would ask the gunner for feedback on his "FO" style. It gave our unit confidence to know that the dialogue was two-way. The gunner was given a shot at calling in a few corrections, so to speak. Let the protégé know you are anxious for the feedback process to work.

It is instructive that the word "feedback" starts with the word "feed." Truly the most optimum gap-filling is that which happens in the spirit of feeding or nurturing. It is also fitting to know that the word "advice" probably originated from the Latin words *mihi visum est*, or "it seems to me." Our words "counsel" and "consult" derive from the Latin *consilium*, meaning "consultation." If we blend these archaic definitions of "feedback" and "advice," we get a perfect description of a learning partnership—to feed together.

Advice and feedback are clear gifts of the mentor, albeit sensitive gifts. They require an attitude of egoless surrender on the part of the mentor in order for the protégé to experience both as gratuitous rather than self-serving. The challenge of all mentoring relationships is the delivery of power-free counsel. This challenge is particularly difficult to meet when giving advice and feedback.

HOW TO MOVE FROM TRAINING TO PERFORMANCE IMPROVEMENT

31

Diane Gayeski

Diane M. Gayeski, *Ph.D. (407 Coddington Road, Ithaca, NY 14850, 607-272-7700, gayeski@omnicomassociates.com), is a researcher, consultant, and speaker in the area of organizational communication and learning systems. Through her work as a partner in OmniCom Associates, she has led over two hundred client projects, involving the examination and adoption of new technologies, models, and organizational structures for training and performance improvement. The author of seven books, she also maintains an academic affiliation as Associate Professor of Corporate Communication at Ithaca College. Diane was also a contributor to* **The 1996 McGraw-Hill Training and Performance Sourcebook.**

Many organizations are looking for new approaches to training and other types of communication such as documentation, policies and procedures manuals, and news updates. This guide provides an overview of how and why organizations are redesigning their training departments, describes several short case studies, and offers some conceptual foundations and practical steps to move from traditional training approaches to a more contemporary performance improvement model.

We read and hear a lot these days about moving from "training" to "performance consulting," about "reengineering" training and human resources, and about establishing new infrastructures for the dissemination of information. Why are so many organizations looking to reinvent their training and communication systems?

✓ Most training and communication systems in today's organizations were designed for old-fashioned top-down management. The traditional assumption was that there was "somebody" who had the information or knowledge to share, and it was the job of training and communication to somehow replicate that knowledge in the heads of employees. The philosophy, technology, environment, and information-dissemination practices in use today generally do not support collaboration, teamwork, or multi-way communication, which are the lifeblood of today's fast-paced and diverse organizations.

✓ Training, information, and documentation have to happen more quickly than ever to be effective and relevant. Traditional design and development paradigms generally can't keep up with changes in policies and products.

✓ Typical systems and practices often foster an "entitlement" attitude among employees with the assumption that if something is important, the company will somehow create a course and tell employees to attend, rather than continuous learning being the responsibility of all organizational members.

✓ Training and communication often don't have much credibility with management; there is little data to prove return-on-investment, and it is generally not tied to business strategy. Training courses, documentation, and manuals also are often viewed with skepticism by their audiences, who often find that the content is not current or supported by their supervisors.

Training vs. Performance Improvement

Although trainers and instructional designers have continuously applied new strategies and media to their work, today's challenges demand even more radical restructuring of the conceptual and philosophical basis of learning. A popular term for this shift is "performance improvement" or "human performance technology." The core idea behind this movement is that training alone is insufficient to bridge most performance gaps, and that trainers need to develop more comprehensive interventions that include incentive systems, communication technologies, environmental redesign, selection processes, and job aids. Using many familiar theories of behavioral and cognitive psychology, translating subject matter experts' knowledge into easily understood concepts, and applying many of the same technologies being used in training, specialists in instruction can broaden their expertise and toolset to create performance improvement projects that are much more powerful.

Although it's not uncommon to hear organizations talk about "reengineering" their training systems, for many this means that they have merely replaced classroom teaching with self-paced CD-ROMs, distance education, or other new technologies. The performance improvement notion implies much more radical rethinking of the whole notion of training and learning. As you'll see in some of the short case studies below, it's not always possible or desirable to create courses of any type. Workplace performance can often be improved by other less costly and more direct methods. Moreover, faster and more collaborative communication systems can increase organizational knowledge and capabilities far more significantly and strategically.

Here are some situations in which organizations decided they needed to redesign their training and communication systems. They are not atypical of many contemporary organizations.

✓ A manufacturer of forklift trucks was rapidly expanding its product line, and thus was also expanding the number and size of manuals for its technicians. Technicians in the field were carrying around some 1,200 pounds of manuals (they needed to order larger trucks just to carry around the manuals, and often could not fit necessary parts on the trucks because the manuals took up so much room!). If technicians enrolled in each of the courses offered by headquarters that related to the product line, they would spend almost one-third of their first two years in the classroom rather than on the job. Despite this embarrassment of information riches, the performance of the technicians was steadily decreasing because the new computerized trucks were displaying unpredictable and complex faults that were covered neither in training nor in the documentation. Technicians were not encouraged to use the help line: The only way they were able to call in was to borrow customers' phones, and even when they called in, the staff were generally unable to come up with an answer. Customers were becoming dissatisfied with truck reliability, and technicians were becoming increasingly frustrated. Neither helped the turnover rate or customer confidence.

The solution to this dilemma was to completely abandon traditional notions that training and documentation could ever completely capture and disseminate all the information that technicians would ever need. The trucks were simply too complex to be able to teach and document everything, and there was no way that technicians could somehow memorize all the procedures and fault codes. In fact, the best information was being developed in the field itself, when complex problems were identified and somehow repaired. Unfortunately, this valuable information was never captured by the manufacturer, since technicians had no incentive to call in and explain how they figured something out. A new, interactive knowledge system was needed to replace the traditional top-down training and manuals.

The company is now building a World Wide Web site that will contain dynamic information that technicians can access in the field via a laptop computer connected via a cellular phone and modem. The information will not only provide the latest information from the factory, but will capture important knowledge from the field. Technicians and dealerships will receive incentives for sharing knowledge, and will become a community of learners, along with the training, documentation, and engineering staffs. While training classes and manuals won't go away, they will be pared down to the basic concepts—while details of troubleshooting will increasingly be built into the trucks themselves and shared via the Web site.

✓ A large international bank found that tellers were actually performing *worse* after going through the basic teller training course than before it. They were apparently being loaded down with so much information that they literally "froze" when they returned to work and faced customers. This classroom training was not only ineffective, it was expensive and cumbersome: The bank's 34,000-person workforce spanned over 4,000 miles, from branches in major cities to remote locations with only one or two employees in part-time jobs. On top of rapidly changing policies and bank products, the bank was completely restructuring its workforce in an initiative that would eventually eliminate tellers' jobs and upgrade them to customer service representative positions. Their new CEO launched initiatives to foster diversity, teamwork, and a customer orientation.

The training department realized that a redesign of not only teller training, but of their entire training philosophy was in order. They commissioned an analysis of their training methods and materials, resulting in a document that defined new philosophies and practices for the training department. These policies aligned the training department more closely with the bank's mission and values, and oriented it to performance improvement rather than teaching. The consulting team not only worked with the training department, but also involved advertising and employee communication professionals on the implications of communicating messages and customer expectations. These crucial inputs provided important links among the various communication providers in the company. As a model of the new philosophy, the former training courses were replaced by a series of short magazine-like training modules, each of which contained opportunities to observe and participate in the actual work and to be mentored by the branch manager and experienced colleagues. "Feature stories" for these manuals were based on actual incidents contributed by tellers within the bank and highlighted teamwork and diversity. A number of job aids were developed to minimize dependence on memorization. This new approach has fostered not only better technical performance, but a new and more consistent culture within the bank.

✓ An insurance company was faced with having to continually update coverage manuals. The manuals had gotten so large that they could not figure a way to number the pages, and could not fit the manuals horizontally on the desks. Training had risen to 10 weeks in length before a customer service rep could ever perform any actual work, and often managers sent new employees back to training because their performance was not up to expectations. The training classes were so long that it was almost impossible to fill customer service vacancies in a prompt fashion, and many individuals left the job even before they had gotten through basic training.

It was obvious that the training and documentation systems needed to be redesigned. If the manuals could be designed to be easier to use and more accurate, training would not need to be so lengthy. A first, rather obvious "fix," was to convert the print manuals to an on-line hypertext form which was easier to search and update. However, more fundamental changes in the concept of training and performance were necessary. The notion that employees had to be "fully trained" before doing any work was questioned and abandoned. Short coaching modules were developed that allowed trainees to go onto the floors and observe, and then practice, simple skills under the supervision of an experienced representative. Self-instructional modules allowed individuals to learn certain concepts at their own pace, and to review complex material once they were on the job. Even more fundamentally, the selection process for customer service representatives was analyzed and changed; skills that were easily taught, like typing, were given less weight than a candidate's ability and enjoyment of explaining complex material to customers. Recruiting and interviewing procedures were changed so that applicants got a better picture of the job requirements, and this resulted in better qualified employees who required less training and supervision. Once the manuals are totally converted to an on-line performance-based system, the training is expected to be reduced by almost half, resulting in significant savings as well as an improvement in trainee morale.

✓ Restaurant managers in a U.S. national chain reported that they were spending almost two hours a day responding just to e-mail updates and announcements—in an organization that demands a high level of contact with customers for its managers. The three-day training course for wait staff had gotten so detailed that many servers left the job before they ever waited on a customer, thinking that they could never learn so complicated a job. Fewer employees were interested in management positions, because it meant having to spend 10 to 12 weeks away from home at company headquarters to go through management training.

This organization is in the process of creating communication guidelines to try to eliminate information overload and help individuals make better decisions about using various media such as memos, e-mail, and voice mail. The basic task requirements for servers and food preparers are being examined, such as the traditional requirement that they memorize a complex system of two-letter codes for all the menu items. Prototype electronic "knowledge banks" are being created that will allow trainers to download continuously updated manuals, and will enable managers to easily sort through and summarize daily news updates. A "pull" rather than "push" strategy for communication is being developed which will focus on enabling employees to maximize their time spent with customers rather than with new information.

✓ The training subsidiary of a European automobile and truck company faced declining requests from internal clients for training. In a period of about two years, their revenue had decreased some 30%, as customers looked for newer and faster solutions to their performance problems. Line managers in factories began to contract for training themselves instead of going through headquarters, or just dropped training altogether. In order to try to maintain their jobs and budgets, the training staff was increasingly recommending more expensive and elaborate courses to their clients, but this strategy backfired completely as they priced themselves out of the market.

In order to remain a relevant and competitive resource to their clients, they refocused their service as "performance improvement consultation." They reorganized their staff to align them directly with business lines and content specialties, and added skill sets in performance analysis and in organizational communication support, such as meeting planning and presentation media and documentation. A major program of staff development was initiated, including bringing in industry experts as mentors and workshop leaders. The staff also began to energetically participate in international associations in training and performance improvement, such as the International Society for Performance Improvement. They are now becoming the experts in knowledge acquisition and management for the company's entire international operations, and are enjoying renewed support from their clientele and management. Moreover, they have become leaders in Europe in fostering the performance technology approach.

✓ The staff development department for a regional healthcare system was so occupied doing time management and sexual harassment training that it had no time left to even consider courses on the new economic realities of managed care and capitation that were necessary to the organization's survival. Not surprisingly, this department received little support from management, and became less and less involved in strategic decisions. Employee morale throughout the company was declining, both because of the uncertainty of the environment, and also because of a perceived lack of credibility of management messages and training.

To remain competitive, it was clear that the organization needed to foster continuous learning not just about new medical technologies, but also about management and economics. The CEO formed a strategic planning team, including representatives from human resources, information technology, media production, staff development, corporate communications, and finance, to develop a plan to implement concepts of the "learning organization" and performance technology. After a four-month period of meetings, study, and mentoring by external consultants, they have received approval to reorganize themselves into a "human and organizational development" team that will provide integrated solutions to performance problems in the organization, identify the skills that the company will need to survive in the new marketplace, and implement individual development plans for all members of the organization, from groundskeepers to the executive team. However, staff reorganization and new projects are only the surface changes that are occurring: A philosophy of valuing diverse opinions, appreciating alternative approaches, acknowledging everyone as a learner and a mentor, and celebrating mistakes as well as successes is being promoted. New infrastructures that will make it easier for employees to collaborate and to communicate with management are being implemented, and methods of performance appraisal and compensation are being redesigned.

Key Concepts

There are several key concepts that provide the framework for all of these new designs:

✓ integrating the various "islands of communication" (Gayeski, 1993) in the organization so that training, employee communications, external communications, human resources, and other key message sources all speak with "one voice" for the organization;

✓ improving the selection and integration of training and communication interventions so that clients aren't ordering a two-day course when a simple job aid or a redesign of incentive systems would be a better solution;

✓ developing methods to analyze return-on-investment for communication and learning projects, and making them part of the organization's strategic plan, rather than a form of "entertainment";

✓ building a fast, multi-way, collaborative information infrastructure that makes it easy to share, store, and index knowledge;

✓ forming a new image and structure for training—one that often integrates trainers with employee communications specialists, human resources professionals, media producers, and even advertising and marketing departments; and

✓ ensuring that the basic philosophies and practices of training and communication are aligned with the organizational culture, goals, and values.

Some of the topics that trainers should become more familiar with in order to implement these concepts include the "learning organization," human performance technology, reengineering, and employee communication. The literature and conferences in these areas provide the conceptual framework that is necessary to move beyond traditional training approaches, and to explain new models to management.

How to Get Started

If you are interested in moving from training to performance improvement, here are some specific steps to take.

1. First, define the current gaps and opportunities that exist. Some of the symptoms of a training and communication system that doesn't work include the following (circle those that describe situations in your organization):

   ✓ Courses and manuals are getting too long and are difficult to keep current.

   ✓ People complain of "information overload."

   ✓ There is no return-on-investment data for training and communication projects.

   ✓ Communication and training aren't currently part of the organization's strategic plan.

   ✓ People feel that organizational information in training, manuals, policies, or employee communications is confusing or not credible.

   ✓ People don't act as if learning and teaching are part of *everybody's* job.

   ✓ There are few standards for "exemplary" performance and analyses of the costs for not achieving exemplary performance for specific jobs.

   ✓ Training, technical publications, employee communications, information systems, and external communication and marketing do not work together regularly to focus and integrate core messages.

   ✓ Training and communication are "event"-based (like entertainment) rather than performance-based; they are measured by audience satisfaction.

   ✓ When managers notice substandard performance, they assume that training will fix it, and they "order" a course.

✓ Trainers and developers are rewarded for how much material they produce, rather than for how much time or money they save.

2. If you notice that even one or two of these are true of your organization, immediately seek management support to examine and improve the system. Don't think that pointing out your own shortcomings will lead to criticism; experience shows that management is also aware of new trends in performance improvement and will be pleased that you are looking for better methods. (Many training departments have been completely shut down and reorganized when their own staffs seemed unable to revamp their own approaches.)

3. Get the support of at least three internal and three external colleagues. You need other employees to add perspectives and endorsement. You need at least one unbiased and well-credentialed expert to echo your views; this might just mean giving some key managers a great book to read or videotape to view, or it might help to bring in an expert to give an executive briefing. Colleagues in similar organizational situations who have successfully adopted some new performance-based strategies will provide a sanity check and a morale boost. Join organizations such as the American Society for Training and Development and the International Society for Performance Improvement (both have headquarters in the Washington, D.C. area). Their conferences and journals will provide ample stimulation and references.

4. Get management endorsement to form a study team or task group. This should be a cross-functional group with representatives from training, HR, employee communication, information systems, and media production. In many organizations, the marketing and advertising departments should also be included. This team should look at what each department is doing to promote performance improvement, and how the various teams could work together more closely. Establish a firm but simple goal and an aggressive time schedule.

5. Execute a prototype intervention. Take a significant organizational performance gap, and with the team, develop an intervention that includes a wide range of coordinated performance improvement activities. Examples of this might be:

   ✓ a prototype intranet (an internal World Wide Web server) that integrates a short training module, company news, and continuously updated news about your industry, linking all these facts and issues into a comprehensive context

   ✓ a new employee selection and orientation system for a certain job, including more appropriate ways to describe the job, interview and select applicants, give them an accurate picture of the job even before they accept it, and then provide a firm context of the organizational culture and mission

✓ a system to reduce waste, including some employee awareness, incentives, and training in the new ways to operate more efficiently

✓ a new computerized sales tool that includes presentation materials that can be customized, along with a coaching guide and product knowledge tutorials and quizzes

Evaluate the return-on-investment of this prototype, and document what you learned that will help you create more powerful projects in the future. Don't be discouraged if this project takes a long time and leads to a lot of infighting and frustration. You will just be learning new skills and interacting with a new team. It's natural to get defensive and to stumble over new ground. Don't give up.

6. Spread the word of your study and prototype undertakings. Gradually make others aware of these new approaches by highlighting courses or professional meetings and by publicizing the success of your intervention. Consider writing up your case study and presenting it at a conference or publishing it in a trade journal.

7. Develop a new vocabulary. Change the name of your department, or at least your job title, to remove "training." When you meet with clients and sponsors, talk about "interventions" or "projects" rather than "courses." Don't refuse to develop training; rather, suggest alternatives or additions.

8. Generate enthusiasm for a new way to do things. Dispel the fear that trainers will lose their jobs, or won't be able to function in new roles. Celebrate successes and accurately reflect how you stand with respect to benchmark departments or professionals outside your own organization.

9. Get the buy-in of at least one top executive. When she or he thinks the time is right, develop and present a white paper with your recommendations for organizational change.

Although these recommendations may sound ambitious, numerous trainers and consultants have applied just these steps to redesign and renew their training departments and individual careers. Although no two results are (or should be) the same, this process has been demonstrated to produce quick and dramatic improvements. As one professional who participated in a four-month intensive strategic planning committee and prototype intervention said, "There's no going back—I'll never do my job the same way again."

REFERENCES

Gayeski, D. and Williams, D.V. (1994) *Tools for Reengineering Training.* Ithaca, NY: OmniCom Associates.

Gayeski, D. (1993) *Corporate Communication Management: The Renaissance Communicator in Information-age Organizations.* Woburn, MA: Focal Press.

Robinson, D.G. and Robinson, J.C. (1995) *Performance Consulting: Moving Beyond Training.* San Francisco: Berrett-Koehler Publishers, Inc.

HOW TO WORK WITH RESISTANT EMPLOYEES

Hank Karp

H. B. Karp, *Ph.D. is principal of Personal Growth Systems (4217 Hawksley, Chesapeake, VA 23321, 757-483-9327), a consulting firm specializing in conflict management, leadership and supervisory training, and executive coaching. He is also on the faculty of management at Christopher Newport University. Hank is the author of* **Personal Power: An Unorthodox Guide to Success** *(Gardner Press, 1995) and* **The Change Leader: Using a Gestalt Approach with Work Groups** *(Pfeiffer & Company, 1995). He was also a contributor to* **The 1996 McGraw-Hill Training and Performance Sourcebook.**

Having trouble with resistant employees? This guide describes eleven tips to help you understand the reasons behind employees' resistance to change, listen to get the information necessary to deal with the problem, and ultimately determine a collaborative solution that will provide both you and your employees with what you want.

Managers have recently had to adopt a whole new way of looking at their organizations. Terms like "paradigm shift," "visionary thinking," and "process reengineering" have come into vogue and are now part of a new global perspective being used to describe larger systems in the working environment. There is little doubt that the time has come for this current perspective as older ways give way to the newer ones. After all, management is "evolutionary," not "revolutionary."

One thing hasn't changed, however, and it is just as important today as it ever was in the early days of the industrial revolution. The problem of what a supervisor ("coach") does when a strong employee ("empowered performer") resists a change ("transformation") still exists. The vocabulary may have changed, but the problem hasn't when it is looked at from the leader's ("steward's") perspective. The bottom-line concern of "How can I get this person to go along with what I want?" is just as vexing today as it has ever been, regardless of what vocabulary is used to describe the situation.

While many of the newer approaches have been very effective in reducing some resistance to change through increasing worker involvement and input, there is still a sizable portion of individual resistance that will always occur in the presence of any demand or change. To know how to work with it requires an understanding of what an employee's resistance is *really* all about.

Resistance is simply an aspect of power and can be defined as "avoiding what you don't want from the environment." That is, it is every bit as much to the advantage of a person to avoid what is not wanted, e.g., not having to review a budget proposal on one's own time, as it is to get what is wanted, e.g., attending a conference in West Palm Beach in February.

Resistance serves a vital function for individuals. It protects them from unsafe or unwanted outcomes. The function of power is to get you what you want, while the function of resistance is to keep you safe and comfortable in the process. Resistance needs to be viewed as a positive function. When it is, it makes little sense to attempt to break it down, avoid it, or minimize it, because the paradox is that the more you attack another person's resistance, the more you *increase* it. Acknowledge the fact that what people resist is pain, not change. If you spend time showing them that what you want will not result in the pain they thought it might, you will have much less of a problem getting what you want from them.

Here are eleven tips to help managers work *with* resistance to what is wanted, whether that be conformance to a change, or a demand for appropriate behavior.

Tip #1: State What You Want As Clearly, Simply, and Succinctly As Possible

The clearer the demand, the clearer will be the resistance that surfaces to meet it. *This is a good thing!* There is no question that the resistance is there, regardless of whether you want it to be there or not. You have no control over this. What you do have some control over is how that resistance is experienced by the other person. Since the resistance is already there, it is to your benefit to have it experienced as clearly as it can be. If the message is confused then the resistance will also be confused. The result is that you now have to contend with the resistance focused on the demand itself, *plus* the natural self-protective resistance that arises out of being unsure about what is going on.

Tip #2: Say It Once and Then Stop

Present a demand in the best light possible. This is the time to really sell the idea, showing what the advantages are for the organization and how this will benefit the individual as well. Once you have done this and any questions are answered, *sell no more.* Any attempt to continue to convince someone past this point will result in a loss of enthusiasm for the demand and a slow eroding of your own credibility. After awhile the thought dawns, "If this is such a good idea, why are they selling it so hard?"

Tip #3: Get in Touch with What You Don't Like About the Idea

No matter how enthusiastic you are about the demand for change or appropriate behavior, or how good it sounds, there is always some element of it that is going to cost you. If you can maintain enough objectivity about the idea to touch the parts about it that you don't like, you'll be in better position to empathize with the resistance that others are going to surface to meet it. For example, perhaps the employee's chronic lateness has to do with the fact that the work is dull beyond bearing. Being aware of that possibility might be very helpful in coming up with some creative solutions to the problem.

Tip #4: Surface the Resistance Yourself

After you have made the demand and it is clearly understood by others, *ask* for their resistance. There are several advantages to doing this. First, it is totally unexpected and you catch the other person a little off guard. Usually people making demands are attempting to eliminate the resistance or are pretending that it doesn't exist. Second, the only choices you have are either to get the resistance surfaced and into the air where everyone can see it, or leave it buried in a dark hidden corner of the resistor's stomach lining. You are always better off getting it out into the open because then, and only then, you can do something about addressing it.

Tip #5: Make It Safe to Resist

Once you ask for the resistance, tell them why you want it. For example, "I like this idea, however I'm not sure how you are reacting to it. I'd really appreciate your being candid with me, since your opinion matters," or "I need to know why you continue to be late, particularly when it is hurting your performance rating and our production record." If you don't make it safe to resist openly, people will resist silently, either by not reacting to the demand, or worse, agreeing to do what you want and then immediately ignoring it. There are two ways you can begin to make it safer for others to express their resistance openly. First, you can begin to make it safer by *never* attempting to talk other people out of their resistance, and second, you can always remember to thank them for their input.

Tip #6: Listen!

The willingness to listen is the single strongest asset you have at your command for effectively working with others' resistance. Unless people are being intentionally perverse, they are telling you why what you want is potentially threatening to them. In fact, they are telling you something deeply personal about their own vulnerability. By being an attentive and active listener, you not only get the information you need to work with the problem, you give a clear mark of respect for the resistor which makes it that much safer for him or her to continue.

Tip #7: Take Notes

If the session is a long one, and/or it involves more than one person, and/or the demand is complex be sure to take notes as the resistance is being surfaced. First, it is a mark of respect and lets the other person know that what is being said is being taken seriously. Second, it will go a long way in not letting you forget what was said. Nothing will kill the process more quickly than being successful in getting someone to surface their concerns and then promptly forgetting about them as soon as the meeting is over.

Tip #8: Explore the Resistance

Once the person has stated resistance to a demand, it's often helpful to explore it on the spot. This is particularly true if the resistance looks like it's more of a "knee-jerk" response than being actually focused on the specifics of your demands. There are two types of resistance that you have to contend with: authentic resistance, which is focused on the demand; and pseudo resistance, which has nothing to do with the demand itself. Pseudo resistance frequently is in response to things like "I resent authority," "I never liked you," or the #1 cause, "You have never given me the recognition I have deserved and by thunder you are going to do it NOW!" You can usually identify pseudo resistance because it doesn't make a lot of sense in terms of what you are asking people to consider. It is also frequently accompanied by a good deal of whining. One simple but very effective tactic for clarifying the situation is to state, "I am not clear about your concern. *What is your objection to the idea?*" If it's authentic resistance, you'll be told clearly and immediately. If it's pseudo resistance you will get some mumbling and then a quiet withdrawal. Note: Do not ask *"Why don't you like the idea?"* This is a challenge and asks the resistor to defend his or her position. You'll be there for days listening to it!

Tip #9: Acknowledge the Resistance But *Never* Agree with It!

Once the authentic resistance surfaces it is important that you acknowledge it, but not agree with it! If you agree with it the game is over and you have lost. For example, the resistor says, "We just don't have time to make the change you want!" You might respond with something like, "I can see where you might have a concern with the new schedule. Is there something we could do to create a little more slack in your present work load?" Not only does this acknowledge the resistor's concern, it allows you to probe the problem and come up with a collaborative solution that will provide both of you with what you want, at no loss of face for either one. One the other hand, if you forget yourself and agree that there won't be time to make the change … you're finished.

Tip #10: Summarize the Meeting

Very few issues of resistance are resolved in a single meeting. However, whether there is one meeting or a series of them, refer to the notes you have taken and recap all the points of resistance that were stated, as well as any agreements or promises that were made. The resulting value is that it reaffirms the importance of the resistors' input; it underscores your respect for their opinion; it allows a final mutual check on what was accomplished; and, finally, it sets the starting point for the next meeting, if there is to be one. This says that you don't have to go back to selling the idea and resurfacing the resistance all over again. Besides, it sets the stage for a sincere and final "Thank you" for their cooperation at this meeting.

Tip #11: Remember That You Are Only Attempting to Reduce the *Needless* Resistance

Keep in mind that no matter how good the idea or how appropriate the demand, each person is going to see it absolutely uniquely. That says that there will always be a range of acceptance and resistance to any change. Some people will resist the idea, no matter what you say or do to convince them otherwise … *and that's okay!* It is really all right that someone still doesn't like the idea, as long as they are willing to give it a chance, or at the very least, promise not to sabotage it. Don't fall into that well-meaning but deadly trap of insisting that we are all in this together and that everyone should like the new change because we are a team and teams do things together. Continuing to respect the other's resistance *after* the idea has been enacted is, paradoxically, the best chance you have of reducing the resistance even more.

Conclusion

Someone important once said, **"The more things change, the more they stay the same"** and nowhere is that more evident than in the field of human development. Regardless of the changes in vocabulary and in organizational structures, it is important to keep in mind that when push comes to shove, all organizational change really occurs between two people, right here, right now. The clearer this perspective, the easier it is to implement the newer and more complex innovations that are impacting today's organizations.

HOW TO USE 33 360° FEEDBACK

David Lassiter

David Lassiter *is the founder and president of Leadership Advantage (17212 Blossom View Drive, Olney, MD 20832, 301-924-2936, GMVK15A@prodigy. com), a consulting and training organization providing programs and technology for improving personal, team, and organizational performance. An international practitioner, David has extensive experience in designing and conducting leadership and team development workshops, as well as providing consulting services in organizational change. He has conducted 360° feedback workshops with thousands of executives, managers, and individual contributors over the past ten years.*

This guide provides an overview of how to use 360° feedback to increase personal and team performance in organizations. It describes what it is and how it works along with guidelines for choosing a 360° feedback instrument. Suggested applications in organizations, strategies for successful implementation, and pitfalls to avoid are also provided.

My first experience with 360° feedback was a life-changing event. I was pilot testing cutting edge tools for improving personal performance at Marriott Hotels. The instrument was an automated feedback tool that measured management and leadership effectiveness. For the first time I was able to see a side-by-side graphic representation of how I, and others, viewed my effectiveness. The results were not what I expected. From my teammates's perspective, I wasn't nearly as cooperative, open, and team-oriented as I believed myself to be. In effect, I was unconsciously creating a barrier between myself and the team. The feedback was, frankly, a shock. Immediately I thought of the many reasons why the data was faulty. As the denial subsided, my mind gradually opened to the information in front of me and the bigger picture came into focus. I became increasingly aware not only of my shortcomings, but of my strengths as well. The feedback gave me unparalleled insight into what was really going on between me and my team and a newfound ability to make conscious choices to improve my performance. To this day, I regularly use 360° feedback to sharpen my professional abilities and personal effectiveness.

So just what is 360° feedback? The term 360° feedback comes from the analogy to a compass: a circle with 360 points of reference used to determine and monitor direction. Its purpose is, first, to gain deeper insight into how we, and others, see our performance and, second, to reinforce those practices that are effective and modify those that are not. As with a compass, 360° feedback is a navigational tool that lets us know when we are on or off course.

360° feedback generates powerful and balanced information on where you stand, where you are valued, and where personal improvement can make you more effective. It can fill the gaps that invariably exist between how you see yourself and how others see you. You can gain information for and evidence of positive change. 360° feedback assists you in becoming more productive and valued in your organization.

Compared to traditional, one-source feedback processes, 360° feedback is significantly more powerful, reliable, and accurate. The added dimension of 360° feedback is its ability to compile multiple assessments from coworkers and contrast that data with your own self-perceptions. Because it comes from a broader base of perception and interaction, it is less likely to be biased or skewed by one person's opinion. Traditional feedback relies heavily on only one source—the boss. In most cases people interact much more frequently with coworkers than with the boss. People also tend to interact differently with their bosses. We are usually more cautious and less spontaneous when dealing with them. Bosses don't see as much of us or our everyday work as do coworkers and customers. Consequently, feedback from the boss, while valid, is not fully representative of a person's effectiveness in the workplace. It can be one-sided, unfair, or even vindictive, as many people know from experience. 360° feedback levels the playing field by soliciting input from a variety of sources; the boss, peers, coworkers, people you supervise, and even customers. The feedback tends not only to be more balanced, but also to be harder to dismiss due to its' broader range of input. As one user of 360° feedback said, "Everybody can't be out to get me."

360° Feedback Answers Three Basic Questions

360° feedback answers three basic questions:

✓ Why should I improve my performance?

✓ What do I need to improve?

✓ How can I improve?

Why should I improve my performance? In today's constantly shifting work environment, the only true job security comes from the ability to continually add value to the organization. Let's be realistic;

we can all improve. In the "Information Age" it is particularly important that organizations and people continually learn and grow. Otherwise, they face stagnation and joblessness. 360° feedback provides solid performance data to employees, no matter what their position or job title. It also allows the organization to scan its strengths and focus its resources on building the skills needed for enduring success. 360° feedback provides reliable data on proficiency and performance ("How am I doing?"), identifies where I need to stay current ("What's my job requiring of me?"), and clarifies where I might need improvement ("What am I not doing so well?"). Without this data, we're operating with blinders on—estimating our contribution based on self-perceptions and occasional, if not rare, feedback from the boss. My personal experience is that the more feedback people have on their performance, the better their effort and results. It's a win–win situation.

What do I need to improve? A good 360° instrument distinguishes which skills, behaviors, or characteristics are most important to a person's job, identifies strengths and deficiencies, and provides a clear picture of how different rater groups assessed proficiency levels. The recipients can see how the boss, coworkers, and those reporting to them view their proficiency and effectiveness. This is particularly critical information for managers and executives because their behavior and practices affect results across teams, departments, and entire divisions.

How can I improve? A worthy feedback instrument will generate "expert" advice based on reliable research and practice, make specific recommendations on what to do, and provide a clear framework for creating a strong development plan. It will not leave users scratching their heads and wondering what it all means, what to work on, or what to do next. People will walk away with a clear picture of what's working and what's not, and a clear, comprehensive, and specific plan to improve their performance.

How Do I Pick a Reliable 360° Instrument? What Should It Provide?

There are many 360° instruments on the market. Some are automated, some are not. Some are easy to use, many are not. Not all of them are worth bringing home. Ill-designed and untested ones can actually be detrimental to your purposes, so be careful. Before you go looking for an instrument have a clear picture of your intended purpose, the target audience, and organizational readiness for it. It's also helpful to know your budget. Quality 360° instruments don't come cheap. Look at them as investments in the organization's future performance. That is what they are. The following is a checklist of what to look for in choosing an instrument:

✓ First and foremost, a 360° feedback instrument should be thoroughly tested for reliability and consistency. That is, it should measure what it says it measures, and do it over and over again with consistency. If it claims to measure a skill such as Planning, it should clearly define what Planning is, and accurately reflect the person's proficiency in performing it. A well-researched instrument will also be normed against a statistically valid database. This provides a reliable answer to, "How high is high? How low is low?"

✓ It should be easy to use, straightforward, and simple. If it's not, you will get resistance to using it, which will make it practically useless. Given the state and direction of technology, I would recommend the instrument be automated for use with a personal computer.

✓ A good instrument should be clearly focused and specific around a particular set of skills, competencies, or behaviors. Anything less will produce vague and hard to use feedback. No one product will be an absolute match for your needs. Some may measure so many items that it gets very confusing trying to sort it all out. Others may have too few. Stay flexible and go with one that comes closest to your organization's requirements.

✓ The instrument should generate *clear, detailed, and personalized* feedback for the user. The more the better. Generalized performance data is a turn-off because it doesn't produce a connection between the recipients and the feedback. Nonpersonal data is easy for users to shrug off as meaningless fluff. A solid instrument will not only be detailed and personalized but will also provide specific suggestions for increasing performance in weaker areas. Expect to see step-by-step recommendations on how to improve in the subject area.

✓ A reputable 360° instrument should be capable of reassessment and not be limited to a one-time use. Multiple usage makes 360° feedback more of a developmental process than a historic event and allows the user to track improvement over time. It also reduces the cost per use. This is an important factor when assessing cost benefit.

✓ A quality instrument will guarantee confidentiality. No one, including the person receiving the feedback, should be able to identify who said what. This anonymity allows for more honesty and candor by assessors. It also helps to protect against recriminations should the recipient not like the feedback and search for someone to blame.

Applications of 360° Feedback

Solid 360° feedback provides hard, actionable data on performance. Those assessed can get their hands around it, do something with it.

And since it comes from people of their own choosing, it is not easy to dismiss the outcomes. Assessees quite often feel obligated to take the feedback seriously even though they may wish to avoid it. Here are several applications of the 360° process.

Personal Development

360° feedback can be used to help employees master the skills needed in their present job or prepare for a new one. It can also be used to gain the attention of those unwilling to listen to verbal feedback. Personalized and graphically displayed 360° feedback has a striking effect on peoples' attention.

Once digested, the information in the feedback report is next used to generate a personal improvement plan based on which skills are most important and in need of development. A good 360° instrument will provide specific, actionable feedback, along with guided, databased development.

Leader-managers find 360° feedback particularly valuable. To be successful, they need to know several things: 1) Are they demonstrating competence in the skills needed to achieve the results for which they are held accountable? 2) Are they using an approach or style with their teams that facilitates rather than obstructs the achievement of results? 3) Do they have the necessary competencies to navigate the uncertain waters of continuous change? Middle managers are often targets of restructurings and downsizings. For them, survival is dependent on their ability to continually add value to the organization. 360° feeedback provides a means of measuring and making sure their contributions are valued.

When framed properly in a workshop, comparative feedback from self and others sparks a hunger for ongoing improvement. I can recall many managers who, having received their feedback and created personal development plans, returned six to nine months later to reassess their performance. They were eager to get more feedback from their teams to see how much they had improved. If there is one thing that is predictable, it's that people love to hear what others have to say about them, though it may not always be favorable.

Team Development

360° feedback can also be used to stimulate team development. Most users of 360° instruments ask coworkers or team members to provide them feedback. This usually piques the coworkers' curiosity. When the assessees share their results (a recommended practice) and request support from the assessors, the team members' interest is aroused even more. The next comment often heard in the team after such a discussion is, "We all ought to do this." It's not far from this point to the question, "How are we doing as a team?"

Some 360° instruments are designed for team use. The individual proficiency levels from members within a team can be compiled to provide a snapshot of the group's skill level. This profile can generate a rich discussion on which skills are most closely tied to the group's goals, and how current skill levels are driving their present performance and results. In teambuilding, using a 360° feedback process allows a team to express its perceptions of the strengths and weaknesses of each member. Properly facilitated, this strengthens the performance and effectiveness of the team over time. The connection of all members to the team intensifies with the understanding of their own and each others' strengths and challenges. Members' value to the team increases as their strengths are used to achieve team-based objectives. As this "teambuilding" unfolds, communication, support, interdependence, and trust tend to increase. The group profile can be used to focus and align individual development plans to a team plan. This has the effect of clustering vs. shotgunning developmental initiatives, producing more concentrated results.

Change

360° feedback can be used to accelerate organizational change and transformation. It can be used across departments or divisions as a way of spotlighting the need for change and hastening the organizational "shift." I have seen major organizations put thousands of employees at all levels through 360° feedback programs designed to reduce horizontal boundaries, and increase accountability and strategic thinking. It's been used to help sweep out the old cobwebs and bring in fresh air to thinking processes. 360° feedback is used to transform cultures by providing hard data on which policies, practices, and procedures support high performance and which don't. It is often a "wake-up" call for people or groups, who have been blissfully cruising along for years without a clue to how others see, or are impacted by, their performance. 360° feedback can be used as a way to identify and elevate the skills needed to thrive in a more competitive and changing world. Some instruments even measure readiness for or resistance to change. Framed within a discussion of customer responsiveness, for example, this can be a real eye opener.

Self-Directed Teams

360° feedback strengthens accountability and self-management. Since self-directed teams are a nontraditional structure, they can use a 360° process to provide objective and reliable performance feedback for themselves individually and collectively. When a person receives high quality, reliable feedback from coworkers, it highlights and reinforces the connection between individual performance and team results. Through a process of self-assessment, teams can identify their developmental needs and provide their own direction for improving the level and quality of their performance. They can also include customers as part of their assessor base for added feedback dimensions.

Learning Organizations

Organizations tuned to success in the twenty-first century know they will be operating in a fluid, shifting environment. They are well aware that knowledge, both individual and organizational, will be a key success factor. In this climate of continuous change, 360° feedback becomes an invaluable tool not only to stay current, but to continually grow the cutting-edge skills needed to thrive.

360° feedback can also be a quick and easy way of conducting training needs assessments. By keeping track of the skills needed and the proficiency levels demonstrated, training departments can rapidly and accurately determine the subject, content, and frequency of their program curriculum. What used to take weeks can now be done in hours.

Perhaps more than any other tool, 360° feedback promotes continuous learning and growth because it is designed and intended for repeated, not single, use.

Strategies for Success with 360° Feedback

Because it grabs people's attention so well, 360° feedback can become part of the new foundation for increased organizational performance. But it's not "pixie dust" that you just spread around. Like most things that increase results, it requires thoughtfulness in its application. Here are a number of do's and don'ts that have proven valuable in utilizing 360° feedback over the years.

✓ Don't force it on people.

✓ Explain what it is, what it does, how it's used, and its benefits to all concerned, continually.

✓ Emphasize confidentiality.

✓ Disconnect it from any compensation decisions (raises, bonuses, etc.)—make it developmental.

✓ Provide information on its purpose and process to assessors.

✓ Conduct structured feedback workshops for feedback recipients.

✓ Spend time with those people having difficulty with their feedback.

✓ Know the instrument you're using thoroughly.

✓ Provide seamless coordination and support for distributing and collecting the assessment instruments.

✓ Make sure your vendor provides back-up support in case problems occur with the instruments or the process.

✓ Be trained in how to facilitate a 360° process. There's more to it than meets the eye.

✓ Align your 360° process with the organization's culture, procedures, and practices. Support and reinforce it.

✓ Use it inappropriately: Take an instrument designed for developmental purposes and use it to reward or punish performance (Performance Appraisal).

✓ Use 360° feedback without systemic support in place. Examples include:

 ✓ No facilitated workshops are provided to support the receiving of feedback.

 ✓ No institutionalized process or procedures are put in place to support, safeguard, and reinforce its benefit to the organization.

 ✓ Lower levels of the organization use it but not the upper levels.

 ✓ No up-front explanation of the process is provided to assessors or assessees.

 ✓ Insufficient administrative support is available to distribute, collect, and process assessment instruments.

✓ Fail to provide support for feedback recipients. More examples:

 ✓ Data is "dumped" on users; no framing or context provided. ("Here, read this and get back to me.")

 ✓ When contradictory or negative feedback is received, no trained facilitator is on hand to help the assessee work through it.

 ✓ When feedback is rejected, no facilitator or coach is available to probe the assessees' resistance, or search for ways to allow them to "hear" the feedback.

✓ Unethical behavior occurs within the organization. Examples:

 ✓ Breach of confidentiality by report processor or facilitator (leaking or talking about a person's results)

 ✓ "Hammering" recipients with their results after they've shared them with facilitator or boss

 ✓ Threatening assessors to reveal how they assessed someone

 ✓ Recriminations against those who provided (or didn't provide) feedback to the assessee

A Word of Caution

Feedback is almost always a sensitive subject. People are often cautious, sometimes fearful, and occasionally emotional about it. A good facilitator or administrator recognizes and appreciates the sensitive nature of 360° feedback and takes serious steps to insure the integrity of the process and support of the individual. Once the process has been breached by any of the above actions, it will be difficult to recover. Spend the time up front doing the homework necessary to make the process successful. The results will be more than worth it.

HOW TO DEVELOP
ACCELERATIVE LEARNING

Kathleen Barclay

Kathleen Barclay, *Ph.D. is the Director of Worldwide Field Training for Sun Microsystems Computer Company (2550 Garcia Ave., Mountain View, CA 94043, 415-786-8017, kat.barclay@corp.sun.com) and a principal in Strategic Visions, Inc. (2590 Reveille Dr., Colorado Springs, CO 80921, 719-488-2005), a firm that specializes in personal, professional, and organizational transformation. She develops strategic plans for the implementation of training departments and consults with companies on creative ways to design and deliver distance learning.*

This guide to accelerative learning presents key concepts and techniques that enable the use of effective adult learning principles in business training. Incorporate accelerative learning into your training programs to help your organization sustain its competitive advantage for the next century.

Accelerative, or accelerated, learning is a generic name for a set of interrelated training and learning disciplines that refer both to a process and to a set of techniques that enable people to learn more efficiently. The foundation of accelerative learning, also written as AL, has been attributed by many to Dr. Georgi Lozanov of Bulgaria who, in the 1960s, developed an enjoyable instructional system that enabled people to use both body and mind at peak efficiency to accelerate their learning. Lozanov's suggestopedia learning system integrated psychological, instructional, and artistic training methods with the concept that people learn best through relaxation, enjoyment, and the absence of tension. In the AL learner-centered environment, focus is on increasing the speed and effectiveness of learning, thereby usually reducing the amount of time needed for training for use in education and business environments.

During this same time period, Knowles developed his theory of Adult Learning Principles. In this theory, people are considered to be constantly striving for self-development and will learn best when what they are learning is relevant to them. Learning is best accomplished when participants are active and all senses are stimulated. Participants learn at their own pace, while receiving constructive feedback in a non-judgmental and supportive environment. AL is a method of effectively implementing Adult Learning Principles. Following is a comparison chart of sample traditional and AL training experiences:

Traditional Instruction	AL Instruction
standard illustrations	mindmaps
emphasis on quiet	intensive use of music/sound
lecture	experiential activities/peer learning
low emotion	excitement in learning
accept learner's state	conditions learner
segmented content	unified/global theme

These concepts are receiving increased recognition in the 1990s as changes in our business environments involve consideration of new training criteria to better enable competitive results while reducing the time and expense of training activity. The training function is coming under increased scrutiny regarding relevance, effectiveness, and the value of investment to today's organization. In an effort to address these issues, corporations have begun to increase the use of accelerative learning techniques in recent years.

The effective use of AL in the business environment consists of several concepts and techniques that increase the capacity to learn with less conscious effort, while also having fun. Following is a format guide to development of courses or materials that embrace the AL methodology.

1. *PLAN the creation of a total immersion environment.* A positive emotional, social, and physical atmosphere provides participants with

a supportive and relaxed yet stimulating learning environment. Action learning gets people physically active and involved while they have fun learning. Themes are used to surround the learning environment with colorful sights, sounds, and things to do. Sensory stimulation may include aromas, large mindmaps or memory maps around the room, music playing, and colored pens for note-taking.

2. *PREPARE for enabling the combination of mind and body for effective learning.* AL instructors promote the use of positive speaking, positive expectation, and positive feedback. States like curiosity, anticipation, suspense, confidence, delight, and exploration help participants to be ready for learning. A learner prep kit or invitation may be sent out to peak curiosity in the coming event. During the course, the instructor should be able to read the present states of participants and know how to elicit target states that allow for connecting the current subject matter to previously learned content and to positive applications. The whole brain is engaged for learning through a balanced use of both right and left brain activities—some imaginative and colorful and some sequential and word-based.

3. *PREVIEW the mindset of the learner.* A traditional business trainer hopes that participants come motivated and ready to learn. An accelerated learning trainer assumes that participants come with many barriers to learning, such as the fear of failure or cultural learning styles and customs, and purposefully plans to overcome them during the learning event. Opening and welcoming activities energize, relax, or focus the attention of the participants. The AL format may consist of an overview presentation of the topic in order to introduce concepts and terminology, preferably through the use of metaphors, analogies, and colorful visuals.

4. *PRESENT content adapted for various learning styles and vary the format of the AL training experience.* Primary preferred learning styles of participants include the visual, auditory, and kinesthetic systems. Secondary styles may include learning by:

   a. concrete experience, abstract conceptualization, global observation, olfactory and gustatory sensation

   b. linear experimentation

   c. inductive, deductive, and intuitive thinking

   d. field dependent/field independent learning

   e. past, present, and future reference

   Memory keys also help vary the instructional format by utilizing musical, linguistic, motor, spatial, and sensory sources to help the learner integrate information. For example, Lozanov used a sequence of active and passive concerts in his instructional formats, made up of specific types of classical music. This *musical technique* or key has been modified for business training, now primarily used during group work and break times. *Linguistic keys* include the use of humor, mnemonics, and rhyme. *Motor keys* consist of role play and hands-on activities. *Spatial keys* are based on the use of the whole learning environment including the room corners, walls, floor, ceiling, lighting, and seating. *Sensory keys* complement the learning styles listed above with aromas, color, sound, props, and costumes.

   Attention to multiple intelligences, derived from the work by Gardner, is a key AL concept for incorporating various formats in course presentation. In a 1979 study on the nature and realization of human potential, Gardner developed his theory of seven intelligences that he believes all people have in different combinations. An AL trainer acknowledges these categories to create content in a learning environment where every participant can have success:

Multiple Intelligences	Sample Activities
verbal-linguistic	lecture, tapes, sharing, reading
interpersonal	group work, partners, cooperative
bodily-kinesthetic	action, movement, simulations
spatial	artwork, mindmaps, environment
intrapersonal	self-assessment, intuition, application
mathematical-logical	problem-solving, prediction
rhythmic-musical	patterns of music, sound, concerts

5. *PARTICIPATE in participant-centered learning that involves learners in decision making about the course, its direction, and methods used for learning.* This develops responsibility in participants and the course may be enjoyed more than those instructed by traditional platform methods. Learners are motivated and participate more in activities they are involved in designing. The trainer changes from being an expert lecturer to becoming a facilitator of cooperative learning in which participants learn from their peers.

Participant engagement in strong emotions is also considered a critical factor in AL for several reasons: (a) emotions can only be engaged if the learner is prepared for learning, (b) emotions are a key to implemented long-term memory, and (c) emotions trigger associations with content. Corporate trainers can achieve positive emotions in learners by employing the AL format of preparing the learner prior to and at the opening of the course, then collaborating with the learner in the process of enriching and integrating learning.

6. *PRACTICE involves the use of pervasive, consistent suggestion and de-suggestion.* AL instructors create positive suggestion through the use of affirmation posters, a friendly environment, positive group interactions, active and passive music for content retention, congruent gestures, tonality, volume, and facial expressions. Active and passive activity is alternated: Peer partnering is followed by an imagery exercise, after which participants role play and then sit and listen quietly to a concert review of the material.

7. *PERFORM the learning in real-world context.* AL strives to present the big picture and how the new learning affects the participants' jobs. Learning is kept contextual through the use of simulations, case study scenarios, hands-on practice, and constructive, supportive review and feedback. Immediate application is key for accelerative learning and measurement is designed to ensure feelings of success.

REFERENCES

Gardner, H. (1993) *Multiple Intelligences: The Theory in Practice.* New York: Harper Collins.

Jensen, E. (1993) *Accelerated Learning for Trainers.* San Diego: Turning Point.

Knowles, M. (1984) *The Adult Learner: A Neglected Species.* Houston, TX: Gulf Publishing.

Meier, D. (1994) *AL Clip Art.* Lake Geneva, IL: Center for Accelerated Learning.

Schuster D., and Gritton, C. (1986) *Suggestive Accelerative Learning Techniques.* New York: Gordon and Breach Science Publishers.

Swartz, R. (1990) *Accelerated Learning: How You Learn Determines What You Learn.* Dallas: Essential Medical Information Systems.

HOW TO CONDUCT EFFECTIVE EMPLOYMENT INTERVIEWS

35

Craig Toedtman

Craig B. Toedtman is president of Resource Development Company, Inc. (402 Wood Drive, Suite 101, Blue Bell, PA 19422, 215-628-2293, rdc@rdcinc.com). The firm is a human resource management consulting firm specializing in building high performance, quality-driven organizations. Craig is a certified Senior Professional in Human Resources and has been appointed by the Department of Commerce to the 1994, 1995, and 1996 Board of Examiners of the Malcolm Baldrige National Quality Award. He was a contributor to The 1996 McGraw-Hill Team and Organization Development Sourcebook.

This guide suggests how you can increase your effectiveness as an interviewer by considering and probing core competencies and behaviors during the interview process.

It is relatively easy to determine the experience and skill levels of job applicants. Standard resume reviews and initial screening by human resource personnel typically result in qualifying certain candidates. But how does a hiring manager effectively determine whether a candidate possesses what it takes to succeed within an organization before any hiring takes place?

Employment interviews are conducted for three reasons:

1. to evaluate a candidate's suitability for a specific opening in the organization;

2. to provide information about the position to a candidate; and

3. to create a good image of the organization, making a positive, lasting impression on the candidate.

As an interviewer, you are presented with what could be the opportunity of your career. This is the chance to make a positive impact on the organization by hiring the best person possible to help you maximize customer satisfaction. And you only have 30 to 45 minutes to accomplish all three of your objectives!

There are four basic skills required to interview effectively:

✓ *Social Ease.* Necessary to put a candidate at ease in a stressful situation.

✓ *Communication Skills.* Important for verbally exchanging information in a professional, intelligent manner that will have a positive, lasting impression on the candidate.

✓ *Judgment.* Required to make an accurate evaluation of the candidates.

✓ *Decisiveness.* Necessary for choosing the best and most suitable candidate for the position.

The Interview

Even interviewers who possess these basic skills can run into difficulty if they are ill-prepared for an interview to take place. Here are specific steps to follow to ensure that your interviews are conducted effectively:

1. **Review the specific job definition or position description.** Take the time to make certain that the position description is current. Have your associates review your intentions to make certain that the position will add value to your organization. Is there a better way to organize? Construct the position to make certain that the candidate will be challenged while making an impact on your customers.

2. **Determine the core competencies required to successfully perform the position.** Consider the extent to which basic skills are required, such as:

   Communicating: What will be the employee's predominant method of communication? Telephone? Memos? E-mail? Who will the employee communicate with? Management? Subordinates? Customers? The public?

   Motivating: Does the position require someone capable of motivating others? Could the employee become a demotivator?

   Developing: Will the employee have the responsibility for developing others?

   Problem solving: Will the employee be faced with solving problems? How big? What is the potential impact on the organization?

   Decision making: Will decisions be required as a part of carrying out the employee's main responsibilities?

   Leading: Is the employee expected to lead others when carrying out projects?

Staffing: Does the position require hire or fire authority?

Planning: Will there be projects that require planning? Is planning routinely required?

Organizing: Does the position require organizing? How much?

Goal setting: Will goal setting and monitoring be required?

3. **Identify the behavioral factors required to satisfactorily perform the job.** Consider using Myers-Briggs or DISC behavioral factor analyses to define specific required behaviors such as:

Energy:	Extroverted or introverted focus
Perception:	Sensing, focusing on the present; concrete information versus
Intuition:	focusing on the future possibilities
Decision making:	Logical, objective thinker versus people-centered feeler
Lifestyle orientation:	Organized, settled judger versus spontaneous perceiver
Dominance:	Response to challenges
Influence:	Influence on others
Steadiness:	Response to the pace of the environment
Compliance:	Response to rules and procedures

4. **Review the candidate's resume/curriculum vitae or application.** Look for patterns, gaps, and accomplishments. Make note of any questions to confirm or validate the candidate's past. Look for distinguishing features of the candidate: What makes this candidate exceptional?

5. **Pick your "interviewing style."** If you desire to have a conversation, you will be asking open-ended questions. These are questions that require more than a "yes" or "no" answer and cause the candidate to discuss issues. On the other hand, if you wish to "interrogate" the candidate, prepare questions that will elicit quick responses. Many interviewers use a combination of styles during the course of an interview.

6. **Develop questions to probe the core competencies and/or behaviors.** These questions should cause discussions that will provide the opportunity to learn as much as possible about the candidate. Your objective is to determine what distinguishes this applicant from all others. What unique competencies or behaviors will result in this candidate maximizing customer value?

   Prepare three to five open-ended questions for your interview, based upon position requirements as well as the candidate's background. For example, to find out if a person is a competent communicator, you might ask: "How do you go about influencing someone to accept your idea?" Or, "How do you compare your writing skills to your verbal skills?" Or, "How should supervisors and subordinates interact?"

For a position that requires an extroverted leader who challenges subordinates to new levels you might ask: "How will you go about establishing priorities in your new position?" Or, "What is your greatest strength, and how will this affect your performance?" Or, "What is your major weakness, and how will this affect your performance?"

By preparing three to five open-ended questions, you are in a position to probe and generate discussions with the candidate to effectively determine how the candidate will perform in your culture. Candidate comments will naturally generate follow-up questions, which you should ask to fully explore a candidate's competencies and natural behaviors.

7. **Schedule the interview.** Allow for 45 minutes to one hour for your appointment, assuming the candidate has been pre-screened and appears to be qualified. This should be uninterrupted time to allow for your full concentration. It is too easy to cut an interview short without allowing enough time to fully understand the candidate. The usual consequences of a too-short interview are a future investment of more time or a hasty hiring decision. Make certain you have taken necessary steps to avoid interruptions.

8. **You're ready!** The job description is complete. You've reviewed the resume or application and noted questions that you need to ask for clarification. You know what competencies and behaviors should be considered. You've developed questions to probe appropriate competencies and behaviors. And, you've allowed for appropriate time to conduct the interview.

9. **Begin the interview by establishing rapport.** Take three to five minutes to "break the ice." Your social skills should be used to put the candidate at ease.

10. **Confirm/verify the qualifications.** Review the resume or application with the candidate to answer the questions identified during your review of the resume. This should take only five to ten minutes, assuming the prescreening was performed effectively.

11. **Determine culture fit by exploring competencies and behaviors.** Use the questions you've previously developed to determine whether the candidate possesses the core competencies and behavior styles that you've determined are necessary for the job. Ask questions that will help you determine if this person will add value and help your organization beat your competition. Expand on the resume and qualifications information and determine what distinguishes this candidate from all others. This should take 20 to 25 minutes, unless you determine there is no fit, at which time you should immediately move to the next step.

12. **Provide a "corporate" overview.** Spend three to five minutes describing the company and position, allowing time for particular questions the candidate might have.

13. **Solicit questions.** Provide the opportunity for the candidate to probe. It is important that the applicant leave with all questions answered to determine the fit from the candidate's perspective.

14. **Close the interview.** Leave the applicant with a positive impression. Discuss what will happen next, so that the candidate has a good understanding of how you will communicate with the applicant. Don't make promises you can't keep. And be certain that you make a commitment to get back to them on a timely basis.

15. **Evaluate and record impressions.** Immediately following the interview, prepare a written summary of your reactions. "What did you like?" "What didn't you like?" By scheduling one hour for a 45-minute interview, you have time to complete this task. Writing down your impressions immediately gives you the advantage of making a decision while the candidate's responses are still fresh in your mind.

16. **Communicate.** Contact the candidate with your decision as soon as possible.

17. **Celebrate!** You have completed an excellent interview process.

Summary and Conclusions

The opportunity to hire a new employee is a chance to bring in a person who can make a major difference in your organization. Therefore, the interview process cannot be taken lightly. Don't assume anything. Review the position description to determine if this is really what you want to do. Discuss the opening with your other subordinates to verify that the function is truly necessary. Decide what adjustments should be made with other positions to make certain that the addition to your staff will have positive rewards.

Take the time to prepare for the interview by reviewing the candidate's background, brainstorming questions, and allowing plenty of time on your schedule for the interview to occur. Planning produces the best results, and interviews are no exception. Make the time to prepare.

Conduct the interview with your company's reputation in mind. You want the candidate to leave with positive feelings about your organization, even if the applicant is not qualified for the job. And remember to allow the applicant some time to ask questions to help her determine if yours is an organization with whom she would like to work. It's a two-way street, and both parties need to explore!

The interview process should be an enjoyable experience for both the interviewer and the candidate involved. Give it the time and importance that it deserves!

REFERENCES

Beatty, Richard H. (1995) *The Interview Kit.* New York: John Wiley & Sons.

Bolles, Richard Nelson. (1990) *What Color is Your Parachute?* Berkeley, CA: Ten Speed Press.

Cauvier, Dennis L. (1993) *How to Hire the Right Person.* Amherst, MA: HRD Press, Inc.

Morgan, Henry H., and Cogger, John W. (1995) *The Human Resource Professional's Guide to Interviewing.* Orlando, FL: Drake Beam Morin, Inc.

Snelling, Robert O. Sr. (1987) *The Right Job.* New York: The Penguin Group.

Yeager, Neil, and Hough, Lee. (1990) *Power Interviews.* New York: John Wiley & Sons.

HOW TO ENABLE EMPLOYEES TO EMPOWER THEMSELVES

36

Cathleen Smith Hutchison

Cathleen Smith Hutchison *is Managing Partner of Metamorphosis Consulting Group (P.O. Box 1147, Cedar Crest, NM 87008, 505-281-4496), a full-service human resources consulting firm specializing in managing corporate change. She is the coauthor of* **Instructor Competencies: The Standards,** *vol.I and vol.II and numerous professional articles. She is a past officer of the International Society for Performance Improvement at international and chapter levels and of the International Board of Standards for Training Performance and Instruction. Cathleen was a contributor to* **The 1996 McGraw-Hill Team and Organization Development Sourcebook.**

"Empowerment is not anarchy, nor is it abdication." So says the author of this guide, who continues by writing detailed instructions on how to make empowerment work for both you and your employees. Follow the advice in this practical guide to get the most out of a very powerful approach to management.

Many managers are afraid of empowerment because they interpret it as anarchy, with employees doing what they want, when they want. Other managers see empowerment as a loss of control over their function. Many others have "tried it" and say that it is doomed to fail, at least in their organization, because employees are unwilling to become empowered—employees don't want to take on additional responsibility. Employees are frequently afraid that they will receive more blame and less credit.

Most of the confusion centers around a misunderstanding of what empowerment really is and what is required for experiments in empowerment to be successful. What is the truth about empowerment? How can you make it work in your organization? Why should you want to try?

Definition of Empowerment

Empowerment is not anarchy, nor is it abdication. It is preparing your employees with the skills, knowledge, resources, and authority to confidently and competently make decisions that affect the organization.

Empowerment is a combination of:

✓ individuals having the confidence, competence, and motivation to act independently within the broad framework of the organization's strategy;

✓ supervisors and managers assisting those actions by removing barriers and providing clear parameters and strategic direction;

✓ an environment that rewards trying new things and recognizes the learning that accompanies action even when it results in "failure."

The following story illustrates the way some managers approach empowerment and why that approach has given empowerment a bad name in many management circles.

A private reported on his first day of duty to the bomb defusing squad of the security forces for the London Underground. His sergeant welcomed him and gave him his first assignment. "Okay, Pvt. Collins, see that black box over there? It's a live bomb. It is set to go off sometime within the next 30 minutes. Go over there and defuse it, soldier!" The private sputtered back, "B-b-but, I don't know anything about b-b-bombs." The sergeant replied, "This is the new London Underground. You're empowered. Just go over and do it. I'll support you in whatever you do. I'll be right over there behind that bunker, if you have any problems. But then I guess I'll hear about them, won't I?"

This is obviously an exaggeration. But many managers of employees with less visibly life-threatening tasks approach empowerment in much the same way.

Rosabeth Moss Kanter, writing in *The ChangeMasters* (1983), states "Sometimes a manager who simply wants to prove that participation does not work will throw a task at an unprepared team and abdicate all responsibility—thereby setting up the whole thing for failure." This is a more typical version of the exaggerated bomb defusing story.

Levels of Empowerment

Managers need to assess the level of empowerment that is appropriate for a given employee and a given task or set of responsibilities.

The level of empowerment may vary from employee to employee and from responsibility to responsibility. Some employees have difficulty with all tasks, some only have difficulty with some tasks. In either case, they require that the manager *do* the task first to demonstrate it to the employee. With a little more experience, employees will need only to be told *how* to do the task. As they gain experience and skill, employees can act with confidence and competence when they are told *what* to do. As they progress further, employees can act appropriately when the manager specifies the *results* that are wanted or required. Next they will know what results are needed when the manager *identifies the need*. When employees are truly empowered, they will be able to identify the need and act appropriately without coaching or assistance from the manager. This level is what is meant by fully empowered individual contributors and "self-managed work groups." This level is where modern employees, managers, and organizations should aim to operate.

All levels listed above must be completed for every project or task, whether large or small. Someone must always:

✓ identify the need

✓ specify the results

✓ determine what to do

✓ determine how to do it

✓ do the task

The difference in levels of empowerment is evidenced by which pieces of the task are completed by the manager and which are completed by the employee on any given project or task. Ultimately, the goal is to develop employees and move them up through the levels of empowerment. Each level increases in complexity from doing the task through identifying the need to do the task. As individuals move up through the levels, they need greater competence, confidence, and motivation. Doing and knowing *what* and *how* requires competence and increasing confidence. *Specifying results* requires both competence and confidence to be reasonably strong. To achieve all levels—*identifying the need, specifying the results, determining what and how,* and *doing the task*—requires empowerment, competence, confidence, and motivation all to be very strong.

Requirements for Empowerment

Studies have shown that there are three areas that must be addressed in order to successfully implement an empowerment program:

1. There are organizational conditions and environmental practices that must be in place, and barriers that must be eliminated or modified.
2. There are leadership and management behaviors and practices.
3. There are individual contributor and team behaviors and practices.

Most empowerment initiatives focus on the behaviors and practices for individuals and teams without addressing the organizational conditions and environmental practices or leader and manager behaviors and practices. These initiatives are likely to fail.

Conditions and Environmental Practices

Organizational conditions and environmental practices center around:

✓ supporting learning for all individuals;

✓ providing clear strategic direction and expectations without restricting actions through tight control, policies, procedures, and structure;

✓ allowing individuals to have input/control over their own destinies; and

✓ developing free-flowing communication channels so that information is shared up and down, horizontally, and back and forth between the customer and the provider.

Organizational barriers to empowerment may vary from one organization to another. However, typical barriers that may occur include:

✓ lack of or inadequate communication

✓ management being unwilling to "give up control"

✓ individuals being resistant to or fearful of change

✓ fear of failure and attendant negative personal consequences

✓ mismatched authority and responsibility levels

✓ restrictive policies, procedures, practices, and values

Conditions within the organization are infrequently addressed by current literature on empowerment, but must be in place for success. This area may be most responsible for the failure of empowerment experiments. These issues should be addressed as a first priority when the organization attempts to instill empowerment.

Leader Behaviors and Practices

Leader/manager empowerment behaviors and practices center around:

✓ creating an environment that encourages competence and confidence, and supports risk taking with positive consequences.

✓ removing barriers to performance (including getting out of the way if they, themselves, are a barrier).

✓ providing clear instructions, context and the relationship of the task to the mission of the team, the group, and the total organization.

✓ encouraging individuals and modelling appropriate behavior.

✓ facilitating career development and enhancement.

Managers need to recognize that you cannot empower someone else. Empowerment comes from within. However, empowerment behaviors must be modeled, supported, and reinforced by the behaviors and practices of the leaders in the organization if they are to begin and/or continue.

Individual contributor and team behaviors and practices center around:

✓ taking initiative.

✓ taking risks with new ideas, new ways of thinking, and new actions.

✓ increasing their own competence, confidence, and motivation to act.

The employees' piece of empowerment is in taking action to move themselves up the levels of empowerment. They must provide their own motivation and internal drive to take action.

The Empowerment Process

Empowerment is a multistep process that addresses all three components of empowerment—organizational conditions, leader and manager practices, and individual contributor and team practices.

1. *Organizational Analysis.* The organization identifies conditions and barriers currently operating that prevent empowerment and action by employees. These could include:

   ✓ organizational factors

   ✓ lack of clarity around strategic plan and direction

   ✓ style of supervision and management

   ✓ reward and recognition systems

   ✓ nature of jobs

   ✓ feedback systems

   ✓ modeling

   ✓ other

2. *Organizational Action Planning.* The organization designs changes that address identified barriers and that will support an empowered workforce. These changes may include one or more of the following or additional initiatives:

   ✓ participative management

   ✓ defining and/or clarifying strategic plan

   ✓ goal setting

   ✓ feedback systems

   ✓ modeling

   ✓ employee training

   ✓ aligning authority and responsibility

   ✓ developing effective communication systems

   ✓ contingent/competence-based reward and recognition systems

   ✓ job enrichment

✓ addressing changeover strategies around the emplacement of new systems that are in conflict with old systems (overt or covert)

3. *Leader/Manager Training and Preparation.* The organization trains its leaders, managers, and supervisors in the behaviors and practices required of them, stressing the criticality of their role in encouraging and enabling empowerment. They are taught how to identify the levels of empowerment and what level is needed by an individual or team on any given task or assignment. They are trained in how to provide the guidance, encouragement, and direction that are needed.

4. *Assessment of Individual Contributors and Teams.* Leaders, managers, and supervisors assess the levels of empowerment of their employees for the tasks and activities they are expected to perform.

5. *Individual Contributor and Team Training and Preparation.* Leaders, managers, and supervisors work to coach, train, and develop the competence and confidence of their employees to move up the levels of empowerment. They may use some of the following tactics:

   ✓ coaching, training, counseling, and modeling behavior

   ✓ successful practice experiences

   ✓ opportunity to practice and perfect skills in real situations

   Leaders and managers are responsible for enabling individuals to have the confidence, competence, and motivation they need to take empowered actions and to understand the value of the expected performance.

   Leaders and managers must decide whether employee lack of empowerment results from individual or organizational barriers. If the barriers are individual, the table on the next page can be used as a guide. If the barriers are organizational, then additional analysis and systemic changes must be addressed by the organization (see Vanguard, 1989).

6. *Performance Feedback.* Supervisors and managers provide feedback, both as advice and as encouragement, using the table and including the tactics in the table on the following page:

   ✓ motivational feedback and encouragement on successful performance and on "successive approximations" of the desired performance

   ✓ advice for future performances

   ✓ verbal persuasion

   ✓ high expectations

7. *Alignment of Support Systems.* The organization incorporates the changes into day-to-day operation and ensures that redesigned support systems are operating. Policies, procedures, processes, and systems that support the new performances are implemented.

If you are enabling individuals around:	Then provide:	Using these tactics:
Competence	Guidance	modeling behavior training coaching counseling advisory feeback
Confidence (believe in the ability to perform)	Guidance Encouragement	practice opportunities (guided or nonguided) "successive approximation" of the task motivational feedback
Motivation (willingness to perform)	Encouragement	high expectations reward and recognition
Value (belief that performance is worthwhile)	Direction Encouragement Guidance	goals and objectives vision high expectations reward and recognition modeling behavior coaching addressing organizational issues regarding negative consequences

8. *Implement Reward and Recognition Systems.* Ensure that reward and recognition systems are in place to:

   ✓ support leaders/managers/supervisors to provide appropriate guidance, encouragement, and direction

   ✓ encourage individuals and teams to take responsibility and initiate actions

9. *Monitor Ongoing Progress.* Assess and monitor individual and team progress toward increased levels of empowerment. Provide individual and team feedback on performance improvement around empowerment behaviors.

10. *Audit Changes to Organizational Barriers.* Audit the organization for progress toward elimination or minimization of barriers and conditions that inhibit empowerment. These changes will not happen overnight and there is often a tendency to revert to old habits. Periodic auditing will identify slippage.

REFERENCES

Kanter, Rosabeth Moss. (1983) *The ChangeMasters.* New York: Simon and Schuster.

Vanguard Consulting Group. (1987) *Levels of Empowerment.* Unpublished concept paper. Larkspur, CA: Vanguard Consulting Group.

Vanguard Consulting Group. (1989) *Leadership Model.* Unpublished concept paper. Larskspur, CA: Vanguard Consulting Group.

HOW TO ADAPT YOUR TRAINING TO DIFFERENT LEARNING STYLES

37

Kimberly Ishoy

Kimberly C. Ishoy *is the project manager of technical insurance training at J&H University, Johnson & Higgins (Four Stamford Plaza, 107 Elm Street, Stamford, CT 06902, 203-353-6224, Kimberly_Ishoy@jh.com). She consults with insurance practice leaders and managers of target markets on training needs to apply learning disciplines in the areas of strategic planning, team development, and organizational change.*

This guide provides practical ideas for fitting training content and interactive learning activities to various learning styles. Strategies are described to avoid the "one-size-fits-all" syndrome in training.

Greek mythology tells us of Damastes, a famous robber of Eleusis. Damastes was also known as Procrustes, which means "the stretcher," because he tied travelers seeking overnight shelter at his place on an iron bed and fitted their limbs to the length of the bed—stretching them if they were too short, and cutting them off if they were too long. It is from this legend that we have usage of the term "Procrustean bed," which describes a scheme or pattern into which someone is arbitrarily forced.

Background

Traditional training environments encourage subject-matter experts to use their presentation skills to persuade or "force" participants to their way of thinking, in effect "tying" the participants to a conceptual form of an iron bedstead, or a "Procrustean bed." The challenge to all who are in a teaching or coaching role, or in any sense facilitators of learning, is to bear in mind that their own learning styles probably dominate their approach to training others and may create the Procrustean phenomena for their participants. Effective training focuses on mastering an effective learning environment, thereby allowing participants to learn in the way they prefer, not necessarily the way we prefer to teach.

The word "education" has its roots in the Latin word *educere,* to draw out. The educative process is to draw out from within the learner what is already within them when they come to the learning experience. The purpose of this guide is to suggest solutions to the complex problem of fitting the training to the participant. The singular solution is to focus not so much on how information is presented, although that is important, but to unfold the nature of how participants prefer to process information.

Through our experiences in schools, universities, and training seminars, we learn what teaching styles we are most comfortable with and which ones make us uncomfortable; which ones conform to our learning preferences and which ones "force" us to lie on a Procrustean bed of information. We feel more successful in the learning environments that conform to our learning preferences, and excel at the subject matter being taught. Our success as trainers is dependent upon our ability to adapt our personal teaching style to the learning preferences of our participants.

Learning Styles

The four learning styles are as follows:

Style A: devoted to getting to the facts; figures problems out logically; uses rational approach; requires factual, solid data; enjoys reducing complex issues to simple decisions; prefers reading materials and verifiable facts

Style B: relies on what has already worked; procedure; order; stability; prefers a well-planned, precise curriculum

Style C: is sensitive to moods, atmospheres, attitudes, feelings, and experience; prefers talking and freewheeling discussion about subject matter

Style D: enjoys originality, ambiguity, and surprise; likes to "turn things upside down"; prefers confusion and chaos; enjoys many possibilities; resists coming to conclusions

These four learning styles explain why such varying reports are received by participants attending the same seminar:

"I didn't like such long discussions—too many choices, no right solution."

"The role playing made me feel uneasy—took too long."

"We were told what to do the whole time; how does it apply to my situation?"

"I've heard this before—it was just presented a different way."

These seemingly conflicting reports can frustrate a trainer. Although these seem to contradict each other, the diagnosis is the same: The trainer did not allow each participant to learn in the way the participant was most comfortable. Since all audiences are comprised of many variations on these four learning styles, all four need to be satisfied in order to ensure an effective learning environment.

Matching Learning Activities to Learning Styles

Since each participant has varying learning preferences, it is important to provide a variety of activities that allow participants to practice and apply the knowledge, skills, and behavior they gain from training. These activities have greater impact when they are adapted to the needs of each learning style. Participants must feel comfortable putting new knowledge, skills, and behaviors into practice in a way that meets their learning needs.

For example, suppose you were putting together a training seminar on employment practices. Below is a list of various learning activities you could ask the participants to do, each resulting in significant learning about this subject, along with the learning style associated with the activity:

1. Reading a book or two on the subject (Style A).

2. Interviewing knowledgeable people in the field (Style B).

3. Attending a series of lectures by subject matter experts (Style A).

4. Writing letters soliciting information and viewpoints on the subject from a range of interested people (Style C).

5. Viewing videotapes or films of people's experiences (Style C, possibly B if it focuses on what has worked).

6. Visiting the Equal Employment Opportunity Commission and acquiring relevant materials (Style B).

7. Participating in a simulation that models the administrative process of settling an employment practices lawsuit (Style B if mostly process oriented, possibly D if creative solutions are involved).

8. Writing a paper, article, or speech on the subject, based on any one of the above experiences (Style D).

9. Role playing to dramatize the contrasting attitudes different employees have about employment practice issues (Style C, possibly D because of the creativity involved).

10. Interning for a week with a human resource professional (Style C).

Participants' preferences among these learning activities, for any given subject, is critical to effective learning. If you can arrange for your training session to involve a variety of learning activities, ones that can be adapted to participants' own learning styles, the participants will find the experience more pleasant and productive.

Let's look at a scenario of three sales representatives of an electronics company trying to learn about the company's latest electronic product:

Angela attended a seminar comparing her company's new product to the competitors' products. She found herself sinking fast in the vast quantities of technical information being told to her, and had difficulty keeping up with the data on competitors' products.

Bart, on the other hand, was struggling to master the product by using the operating manual. "I felt mired in details in the manual," he explained. "I couldn't really get hold of the big picture, so all those details kept slipping away."

At the same time, Nancy wanted to learn how to market the new product for an upcoming trip to a trade show. She felt uneasy with the "scraps of knowledge" she was accumulating from the assortment of promotional books and pamphlets she was given.

Each of the sales representatives' learning difficulties were caused by their different learning styles:

✓ *Angela preferred learning technical information through reading. Once she acquired the operating manual, her questions were satisfied.*

✓ *Bart preferred to learn by talking to others in the field. His problems were readily solved when he called the manufacturers' 800 number, explained the situation he was dealing with, and was referred to a technical consultant.*

✓ *Nancy preferred originality in presentation. She felt much more comfortable about the upcoming trade show once she was able to role play different sales approaches with different types of customers.*

What does this mean to you? It reflects the simple truth that you can make your teaching more productive by capitalizing on your participants' learning styles. Like these three typical learners, you can make learning easier for your participants and more productive by providing learning activities that reflect how they like to learn.

Sample Learning Activities

The possibilities for learning activities are endless. Listed below are a few initial suggestions that can be utilized as pre-course work, learning activities during the course, and as post-course follow-up:

Learning Style A

1. Read articles, books, manuals, promotional materials
2. Analyze the risks, possible options, potential outcomes
3. Create an action plan, PERT, or GANTT chart
4. Analyze case studies
5. Write an article on the subject matter

Learning Style B

1. Attend a lecture/presentation
2. Talk to others who are experienced about what works
3. List the pros and cons
4. Receive tutoring/mentoring from another experienced person
5. Observe another who has the skill, knowledge, or behavior

Learning Style C

1. Brainstorm with others
2. Keep a daily journal about things tried, successes, and failures
3. Receive feedback from others
4. Emulate behavior of another person
5. Talk with boss, peers, direct reports to get ideas

Learning Style D

1. Role play scenarios
2. Learn by doing/trial and error
3. Reflect on similar past events, searching for historical parallels and analogies
4. Create a list of best practices from own experience
5. Analyze case studies with no clear solution

Conclusion

No one learning style is better than another; each has its strengths and weaknesses. No learner falls into the same learning style all the time; each of us has dimensions of each style, yet predominantly favors one over the others. Each learning style must be satisfied in order to ensure learning retention for each participant. The challenge is to incorporate many diverse learning activities into training scenarios that meet the needs of each learning style in order to maximize effective learning. Beware of the one-size-fits-all, "Procrustean bed" approach to training and instead work to fit the training to the participants.

HOW TO ENGINEER A SUCCESSFUL COMPETENCY/ CAREER MANAGEMENT SYSTEM

Mary Keller

Mary T. Keller *is the Training Coordinator for Boehringer Mannheim Corporation (BMC, 2400 Bisso Lane, Concord, CA 94524, 510-674-0667, mary_keller@boehringer-mannheim.com). She is responsible for managing training and development at the Concord site, and specializes in competency/career management systems.*

This guide uses the concepts of knowledge, skills, and attitudes as its foundation to build a competency/career management system. The five tools of the system can assist managers in their efforts to consider employee competencies as a pool of resources, while helping employees to develop and further their own careers.

Organizations, especially those in high technology industries, are faced with pressure to be nimble responders to market demands if they are to survive. Training and development functions have a responsibility to help their organizations build this competency. This implies strong development and cross-training of employees. A competency/career management system can help organizations be responsive to changing needs for knowledge and skills and can help their managers and employees acquire and manage their new knowledge and skills.

Employees have different needs to be met by a competency/-career management system, depending on the role they play in the organization: management or nonmanagement (employees). The system should be designed so that it speaks to its users in a common language they can understand and provides tools that accommodate varying needs. This shared way of talking about the system and using its tools is a "commonspeak."

The concepts of Knowledge, Skills, and Attitudes (KSAs) provide that common language. These three pieces of training bedrock can be positioned to your organization's management and employees in ways that excite their interest in your system and give them each a customized way of getting what they want out of training. Using KSAs as a foundation links well with efforts to establish succession planning and a compensation structure, which includes pay for skill.

A competency/career management system (see Figure 38.1) built on the KSAs foundation contains these tools:

1. Job Descriptions
2. Position Training Plans
3. Training Documentation System
4. Learning Transfer Plans
5. Individual Development Plans

The tools are meant to be used in combination with each other, although any tool can stand alone.

A performance evaluation process should also be incorporated into the system. Each tool is discussed separately, including its use and benefits. These benefits serve as selling features of the tools as you roll out the competency/career management system in your organization.

Competency Management or Career Management?

The success of a commonspeak system depends in part on how well it addresses the needs of the people who use it. Managers have a need for tools to help them meet business needs and supervise their employees. Employees have a need for growth opportunities and advancement, and a need to be valued by the organization. As you introduce the system, train management and employees on its concepts and use. Highlight these aspects:

Commonspeak System: Benefits and Uses

For Management	For Employees
✓ Functions as a competency management system: a collection of tools and processes that help in managing KSAs as a pool of resources ✓ Responds to changing work priorities	✓ Functions as a career management system: provides support for building and using new KSAs ✓ Ensures development opportunities ✓ Clarifies development expectations

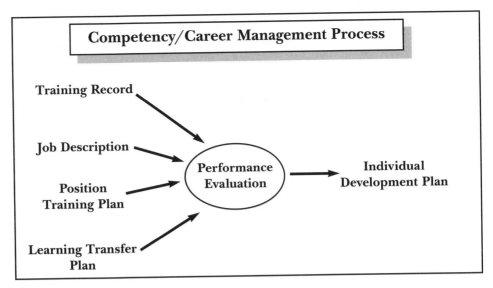

Figure 38.1.

An annual performance evaluation should punctuate the ongoing process of competency/career management. The evaluation provides a milestone for evaluating past performance and setting training and development goals for the coming year. The goals become part of the Individual Development Plan. (See Figure 381)

1. Job Descriptions

A job description should be used to clarify the job's general functions, competencies needed, competency linkages, and level of decision-making authority. The competencies, or KSAs, listed in a job description form the foundation for developing a corresponding Position Training Plan (see Figure 38.2). Design job descriptions so they are descriptive (What does the job entail?) and prescriptive (how should the employee in the job perform?). Descriptions must reflect the reality of a job and flex with the changing needs of the organization. A job description should also function as a set of guidelines for the performance expected of an employee doing that job.

If you are creating new job descriptions, involve employees in the process wherever possible. If you are working with existing job descriptions, revisit them to ensure they reflect what people in those positions do.

Suggested Sections of a Job Description:

✓ Job Title

✓ Functional Area of Job

✓ Purpose of Job

✓ Job Functions and Contributions

✓ Competencies (KSAs)

✓ Decision-making Level of Authority

Job Descriptions: Benefits and Uses

For Management	For Employees
✓ Functions as a benchmark for assessing whether employees currently possess the competencies that enable them to perform their job ✓ Functions as a benchmark for assessing employee readiness for advancement ✓ Links competencies with the different job functions they support	✓ Identifies which general competencies are needed to be qualified for a position ✓ Clarifies the main areas of job performance and job outputs ✓ Links competencies with the different job functions they support

2. Position Training Plans

A Position Training Plan (PTP) is a list of the training and development activities that an employee should complete to be minimally competent in a given position. There are three sections in a PTP: Knowledge, Skills, and Attitudes. If your organization has specific training programs in place, you may list these as the training requirements for the position. If you do not have formal programs or the specific names of the programs, you can list, for example, the skills that an employee in that position should possess. Next to each skill, list the suggested learning channels. For example, in the knowledge section for a Chemist's PTP, you might list Advanced Laboratory Skills, with learning channels of OJT, Workshop, and Coaching. A choice of learning methods allows flexibility in how, when, and where the training is done. The focus is on acquiring proficiency in that skill.

Learning channels are the different types of training and development activities employees can use to acquire KSAs. The channels are listed below and appear on the Position Training Plans and Individual Development Plans. The channels also help employees to see other options for learning besides formal workshop training. This list may be changed to fit your organization's culture.

OJT	On-the-Job Training
A	Assignment, Project
M	Mentoring, Coaching
W	Workshop, Class
C	Continuing Education
S	Self-Directed Study

An example of a Skills page from a PTP for an Administrative Assistant is shown on the next page.

Administrative Assistant II
Position Training Plan

Department: <u>All departments</u> _____

Skills

Training/Education	Learning Channel	Comments
Advanced word processing software use	OJT, W, S	
Advanced spreadsheeting software use	OJT, W, S	
Basic desktop publishing, including design, layout, and software use	OJT, W, S	
Intermediate alphanumeric filing	OJT, W	
Advanced verbal communication	M, W	
Basic math skills, including data analysis	OJT, W	
Organizing and prioritizing	OJT, A, W	
Advanced proofreading	OJT	
Functioning as a team member	A, M, W	

```
List what is required in each of these        Skills
areas for an employee filling this position    ✓ Technical        ✓ Management/
to be minimally competent in performing        ✓ Communication       Supervisory
the job:                                        ✓ Interpersonal     ✓ Team
                                                                    ✓ Training
```

Figure 38.2.

A PTP should have a corresponding job description. In a job description, the competencies are usually stated in general terms, combining related competencies into one category. In a PTP, competencies are split out such that KSAs are listed separately. To create a PTP, use the job description as a starting point and include input from managers about the realities of their employees' training needs. A PTP identifies minimum training requirements for an employee to be qualified to perform the job. It also functions as a guideline for managers to determine which KSAs an employee needs to develop as part of a customized training and development plan. Some of the training requirements listed in a PTP may be waived or not required if the employee has demonstrated competency.

Position Training Plan: Benefits and Uses

For Management	For Employees
✓ Determines training needed by an employee as part of a customized training and development plan	✓ Identifies which KSAs/training you need to remain qualified for your current position
✓ Ensures consistency in training requirements for employees in the same job	✓ Identifies which KSAs/training you need to become qualified for the next level or a different position

3. Training Documentation System

A training documentation system tracks the training and development activities that help qualify employees to perform their jobs and prepare them for future jobs. It also helps meet the requirements of element 4.18 (Training) of the ISO 9001 standard. You should use a training documentation system that functions as an indispensable tool for these three internal customer groups: employees, managers, and the training function. When you institute the system, sell the tool differently to each group.

Training Documentation System: Benefits and Uses

For Management	For Employees	For the Training Function
✓ Tracks employee training activities	✓ Documents qualifications for current job	✓ Provides data for tracking and analyzing trends in training
✓ Provides information for an employee's annual individual development plan	✓ Documents inventory of KSAs as evidence of promotability	✓ Functions as a budgeting tool
✓ Helps identify gaps in training completed by employees	✓ Documents progress made toward gaining depth in KSAs of current position	✓ Supports Element 4.18 of ISO 9001 Standards
✓ Tracks consistency of training for groups of employees with the same job		
✓ Functions as a cost accounting tool		

Depending on the size, needs, and culture of your organization, paper and/or electronic documentation may be appropriate. At the Boehringer Mannheim site in Concord, California, employees maintain their own training records using a standard form. Records are collected quarterly and the information is input into an electronic database from which reports are generated. Figure 38.3 shows an example of a training record form.

Employee Training and Development Record

PRINT		Training Quarter	
Employee Name	_____	(Q1, Q2, Q3, Q4)	_____
Department	_____	Dates	
Supervisor	_____	mo/day/yr to mo/day/yr	_____

Course/Procedure/Instrument PRINT OR TYPE	Date(s) of Training mo/day/yr	Total # of Training Hours	Cost of Training IT or $	Instructor Signature or Certificate of Completion ✓ if certificate is attached	Trainee Signature

Figure 38.3.

4. Learning Transfer Plans

The Learning Transfer Plan (LTP) is, first and foremost, a tool for continuous improvement. By applying new learning on the job, an organization can improve areas such as job performance, processes, and communication. The LTP is a written plan that identifies the new skills and knowledge an employee acquires through training and specifies how they are to be used on the job. The employee and the supervisor create a mutually agreed-upon plan. The process requires that the employees clarify their goals and objectives for attending a workshop before they attend, and that the supervisor be aware of those goals, modifying them if needed. The LTP closes a gap in accountability: Supervisors know who in their group are spending what time and money on training and the employees know they will be held accountable for applying their new KSAs on the job. The LTP also identifies what sort of obstacles employees might encounter in trying to use their new skills on the job and ways to ensure a successful transfer. An example of a learning transfer plan is found in Figure 38.4.

Learning Transfer Plan

Name _____ Department _____

Supervisor Signature _____ Date _____

Title of Training/Education _____ Date of Class _____

	New Skills or Knowledge #1	New Skills or Knowledge #2
(A) Goals and objectives for attending training		
(B) Plan for on-the-job application		
(C) Resources and support needed		
(D) Results expected from plan		
(E) Evaluation methods		

Complete (A) BEFORE enrolling in the class.
Complete (B) - (E) AFTER completing the class.
Figure 38.4.

The general process for completing a Learning Transfer Plan is:

Step	Process
1	The employee and his or her supervisor complete Part (A) before the employee attends the workshop. They identify the reasons and general objectives for attending.
2	Within one week after returning from the workshop, the employee completes the rest of the LTP, Parts (B) to (E) in conjunction with the supervisor. Part (B) should include a time frame for implementation.
3	The plan is implemented, including evaluation of results.

As with the other tools in the competency/career management system, you will need to train employees and managers on the value and use of the LTP.

Learning Transfer Plan: Benefits and Uses

For Management	For Employees
✓ Helps determine ROI for training	✓ Clarifies intent for attending a workshop
✓ Helps allocate training funds appropriately	✓ Determines level of support that can be expected for applying new skills on the job
✓ Identifies in advance new KSAs needed by an employee for a special assignment or project	✓ Ensures the availability of opportunities and resources to apply and develop new KSAs
✓ Integrates with creating an individual development plan	✓ Functions as written proof of efforts made to increase depth and breath of KSAs
✓ Helps ensure planned growth of the KSA resource pool	

5. Individual Development Plans

The Individual Development Plan (IDP) is a written plan of an employee's training and development goals and activities for one year (see Figure 38.5). It should be completed immediately after the employee's annual performance review. The IDP lists learning activities that aim at improving the employees' current performance, supporting their advancement potential, and furthering their career goals. It also makes a critical link between department goals and employee development goals. As a tool for managers, the IDP helps them manage the competencies of their group as a pool of renewable resources. For example, a manager can use IDPs as a project planning tool to identify and develop KSAs needed by employees in a future project.

An IDP is not written in stone. It is a plan and should be adjusted to changes such as an employee's transfer to another department, new job responsibilities, or a shift in the employee's ability to fulfill the plan. An IDP should allow flexibility in the types of development activities available to employees: workshops, coaching, OJT, self-directed study, and others. This flexibility accommodates individual learning styles, work environments, budgets, and time limitations. Figure 38.5 is an example of an IDP.

Individual Development Plan

Time Frame: <u>April 1996–March 1997</u>

Employee	<u>**Eugene Catry**</u>	Department	<u>**Operations**</u>	Supervisor	<u>**Maria Gonzalez**</u>
Job Title <u>**Administrative Assistant I**</u>					

Department goals relevant to job	General employee development goals
✓ Complete ISO departmental documentation ✓ Produce quarterly metrics reports on kit packaging to track scrap	✓ Improve word processing skills to an intermediate level ✓ Improve proofreading skills ✓ Develop prioritization and organization skills to level of needing minimum direction

Training and Development	Learning Channel	Expected Date of Completion	Estimated Duration of Training	Estimated Cost	Learning Transfer Plan Due Date
Intermediate MS Word class	W & S	May 30, 1996	8 hrs	$150	Jun 2, 1996
Proofreading skills class and special projects	W & A	Aug 1, 1996	16 hrs	$120	Aug 3, 1996
Work on prioritizing daily tasks, especially typing projects Mentors: Supervisor and an Admin. Assistant III	M & OJT	Oct 1, 1996	20 hrs	–	–

Possible Learning Channels

OJT -	On-the-job Training	W -	Workshop, class, or seminar
A -	Assignment or Project	C -	Continuing Education (certificate or degree program)
M -	Mentoring or Coaching	S -	Self-directed study

Employee Signature	Supervisor Signature	Date

Figure 38.5.

The general procedure for completing an Individual Development Plan is:

Step	Procedure
1	Department goals relevant to job: List goals that the employee will be supporting.
2	General employee development goals: List areas of development needed to prepare the employee for supporting departmental goals. List career/growth goals, including long- and short-term goals.
3	List the training and development activities for the year, spreading them out over time. Include due dates for LTPs.

Individual Development Plan: Benefits and Uses

For Management	For Employees
✓ Identifies KSAs needed to support department/group goals	✓ Clarifies manager's expectations for employee's development
✓ Assists in budgeting money and time for training	✓ Supports career growth
✓ Clarifies employee's expectations for personal development	✓ Provides a forum for discussing career/growth goals
✓ Functions as a written plan of accountabilities	✓ Clearly details development activities for the year
✓ Establishes a link between annual performance reviews	
✓ Reinforces the employee's value to the organization	

Conclusion

A successful competency/career management system will help everyone in your organization be better able to respond to changing demands for new competencies. By using a common language and set of tools based on knowledge, skills, and attitudes, managers can effectively deploy their pool of competency resources, and employees can manage their careers. The system encourages strength through diversity. As employees become more diverse in their KSAs, they increase their employability and value to organizations. In turn, the organizations gain the flexible, cross-functional workforces, it takes to grow the business. It's a winning situation all around.

HOW TO CREATE PROFESSIONAL FACILITATOR MANUALS

39

Bonita Sivi

Bonita Sivi *is a managing partner at Thomas Baker Associates (31640 Wekiva River Road, Sorrento, FL 32776, 352-735-1030, tbaker@digital.net). Boni has worked in both education and industry and specializes in management and team development and executive coaching. In addition to creating her own facilitator manuals, she is the current President of the Central Florida Chapter of ASTD.*

How many times have you tried to facilitate a discussion group or conduct a full training program from a collection of hand-scribbled notes? The notes might not have even been written by you. Often "cheat sheets" are passed down from one trainer to the next, with each person adding to or subtracting from the original text. Read this guide to discover how you can change haphazard notes into a consistent, comprehensive facilitator manual that ultimately saves everyone time and money.

Every day in organizations around the world, training programs are presented for the first or fortieth time from a developer or presenter's handwritten notes. Training program documentation for programs developed in-house is often woefully nonexistent. Even in many large organizations, established programs are not well documented.

Creating facilitator manuals from the conception of a new course or for ongoing courses can strengthen your organization or your consulting business. Transferring your learning to others saves effort and expense as your organization is continually asked to do more with less.

Training and development professionals are role models for increasing learning and performance in their organizations. As proponents for the rapid transfer of learning and creation of high performance standards, it only makes sense that they should apply these same principles to their training manuals.

Practitioners must look at systematic ways to transfer knowledge, especially in their own functions, in order to have credibility with the rest of the organization. Practitioners who can effectively transfer their skills through tools such as facilitator manuals are ready to supply line management with what is needed to convert organizations to learning cultures.

Advantages of Facilitator Manuals

There are many advantages and benefits to look forward to with your own professionally created facilitator manuals.

1. Programs are easy to present on successive occasions.
2. Facilitator manuals become living documents that are changed and adjusted for a given situation.
3. Programs that are true to their original design are more likely to be presented consistently to various groups by different facilitators.
4. Content changes are easy to implement.
5. Programs can quickly be transferred to new facilitators.
6. Program presentation can be moved to line management without providing extensive training.
7. Preparation time is reduced for infrequently conducted programs.
8. Knowledge and work accomplishments from former trainers are retained after personnel leave organizations.
9. Team facilitation is smoother as each facilitator knows exactly his or her role. The facilitator team appears very competent to the participants.
10. Program preparation is simple since the list of required materials is always up to date and available at the beginning of the facilitator manual.
11. Trainers in different geographical locations receive consistent information.
12. Manuals for programs on many subjects can quickly be customized for internal and external customer needs.

Eight Steps to Developing Facilitator Manuals

The task of creating facilitator manuals can be broken down into these stages:

1. Transcribe your handwritten notes to a good word processing application program that can later be placed into a desktop publishing program.
2. Print the text if you are not comfortable working directly on the computer. Proofread the information, adding details where nec-

essary. Imagine that someone other than you is going to be presenting the program. If two or more of you are already presenting, have all contributors review the notes, adding details where necessary. Be sure to create a list of all items needed to make the program go smoothly.

3. Add the new details to your text. Integrate ideas into sections you've decided to change because of input from previous participants.

4. The next time you present the program, jot down any notes that come to mind that might make the manual more useful to yourself and others. Be sure to add times beginning with 0:00 and progressing to the end hour, say 4:00 for a four-hour session. You can then add to the start time of the session to know where you should be at any given time. For a specific session, you can even print a copy of the manual that adjusts all times for that particular group.

5. Add the time sequences and new details to your facilitator manual.

6. Print your facilitator manual and study it. Make a list of the types of activities that occur in your program. Your list might include lectures, videos, audiotapes, transparencies, references to a participants' manual, group activities, and other unique aspects of the program.

7. Transfer your script to a desktop publishing program, leaving a wide left-hand margin. One-fourth to one-third of the page should be sufficient. You may also want to put the text in a size 18 font so that you can read it clearly but not obviously when presenting. Naturally you need to know the program well so that participants are not turned off by your reading. Select a symbol or icon for each of the types of activities that you identified in step 6 above. You will be using the icon in the left margin to quickly identify activities while presenting. Place the icons in the margin appropriately.

8. Next create readable graphics miniatures of all the materials you reference while presenting—participant manual pages, transparencies, other reference material. Place them into your script appropriately. This can be challenging to those of you who are not desktop publishing experts. Even many expensive commercially-produced facilitator manuals do not have this feature, but it is very valuable. It contributes to a very professional presentation that avoids paper and booklet shuffling.

Key Sections of a Facilitator Manual

Organizing facilitator manuals so that they can be used effectively is very important. The key sections of a facilitator manual might include:

1. *Introduction*

   This section can be short if you are assuming the facilitator is experienced. It can be very long and detailed if you would like to give information on presentation and facilitation skills that an entry-level person would need.

2. *Materials Needed*

   Be sure this section is complete and descriptive. It can be very helpful to the facilitator.

3. *Prerequisite Information*

   Your facilitator manual might include many training modules, in which case it might be necessary to describe which modules are prerequisites of others.

4. *Summary of Technical Needs*

   This section becomes even more important as technological options increase.

5. *Main Script*

   a. Times

      Describing times for completing sections of modules makes the manual more useful when modification is required. It is very useful, too, for on-the-spot tailoring when time crises occur.

   b. Room for Notes

      This allows updating of the facilitator manual, which is so important to its ongoing usefulness.

   c. Visual Markers (Icons)

      This allows the facilitator to find when the next transparency or the video player is needed. It also allows the facilitator to quickly look for balance in the methods used to train participants.

6. *Additional Reference Materials*

   Give the facilitators all the information they need to be experts.

7. *Bibliography*

   A list of books and articles used to develop the facilitator manual can be helpful to facilitators.

Desktop Publishing Considerations

If you're not an expert in desktop publishing, decide whether you have the interest and commitment to learn how to do it yourself or if you would feel more comfortable paying for a professional's help. Consider the following when deciding on a system to create your facilitator manuals:

1. What type of computer and printer do you currently have? What hardware do you need to support your facilitator manual project?

2. What software do you have available? What software can you convince decision makers to buy?

3. What learning is required to bring you up to speed so that you can create the very best facilitator manuals? What training should you attend and how much does it cost?

4. What desktop basics do you need to learn so you can do the work yourself or check the work of the person to whom it is assigned? Would you be interested in learning desktop basics so you can advise your desktop publisher?

HOW TO LINK EVALUATION TO THE BUSINESS NEED

Susan Barksdale and Teri Lund

Susan Barksdale *is the founder of Front Line Evaluators (25-6 NW 23rd Place, #412, Portland, OR 97210, 503-223-7721), a training consulting firm specializing in evaluating training effectiveness. Susan conducts return-on-investment evaluations for performance improvement initiatives and conducts instructional materials audits.* **Teri Lund** *is a partner in the firm Baldwin & Lund Services (4534 SW Tarlow Ct., Portland, OR 97221, 503-245-9020), which provides consultation in performance improvement methodologies for training professionals. Teri conducts return-on-investment evaluations and develops evaluation strategies.*

How do you really know if your projects and programs improve your organization's bottom line? Read this guide to learn more about the process of linking the business need for performance improvement to the need for evaluation.

Is the Evaluation Needed?

The main reason for evaluation is to determine the effectiveness of a training program or performance intervention. When you complete an evaluation, you hope that the results are positive and gratifying for the sake of those participating in, responsible for, and supportive of the program or intervention.

Specific reasons for evaluating training and performance interventions such as Computer-Based Training (CBT) or an Electronic Performance Support System (EPSS) include but are not limited to the following:

✓ to determine whether a program or intervention is meeting the original objectives;

✓ to identify improvements for a program or intervention;

✓ to determine if there was a return on investment (ROI) for a program or intervention;

313

✓ to decide who else might benefit from the program or intervention;

✓ to test the clarity and validity of tests, questions, and exercises if it is a training program;

✓ to identify who in the organization and/or what process or task benefited the most or least from the program or intervention;

✓ to gather data for planning distribution and/or marketing of future programs or interventions;

✓ to determine if the program or intervention met the business driver and performance need; and

✓ to establish a database that can assist management in making future decisions.

Before determining whether an evaluation is necessary, you must discover the root cause of the problem that originated the request for a training or a performance intervention.

Determining the Causes of the Performance Problem

Performance needs usually drive a project, training program, or performance intervention. These same performance needs should drive the evaluation approach. Optimally you would identify the performance need and the evaluation strategy that measure the effectiveness of the intervention during the analysis stage, which takes place prior to project initiation. However, recognizing that this does not always happen, you must determine what the performance need is or was that is driving the project implementation prior to evaluation.

Also keep in mind that not all causes of performance problems are indicative of the need for training or can be solved by training. During analysis you may discover that both the problem and the solution are multifaceted.

The most common causes of performance problems include:

✓ a lack of skill and/or knowledge;

✓ reengineering or reorganization;

✓ a changed environment (new computer systems, new procedures);

✓ a lack of motivation, downsizing, and/or "survivor's guilt";

✓ new products or major changes in product or service lines; and

✓ a lack of direction or expectations.

If the project is to succeed, it must be part of an integrated solution that uses a variety of training methods and performance interventions and provides support for changes in the environment. Some interventions for the performance problems mentioned above include:

Performance Problems	Interventions
A lack of skill and/or knowledge	Training, job aids, coaching
Reengineering, reorganization	Revised policies, training for supervisors, incentive and bonus plans
A changed environment	Work redesign, new/better tools/equipment, training to use tools
A lack of motivation, downsizing, "survivor's guilt"	Increased communication, coaching training, use of mentors and role models
A lack of direction and expectations	Increased communication, coaching training, use of mentors and role models

Business Drivers

Once you identify the performance need, the next step is to identify the business drivers that were responsible for initiating the project. You may also have to determine if these business drivers still exist and how they have or have not been impacted as a result of the project, program, or intervention. Common business drivers include:

✓ *Economic Drivers* such as recession, inflation, or a shortage of supply of raw products.

✓ *Human Resource Drivers* such as too few resources with particular skills, a shortage of workers in total, or the need to have a more balanced work and family lifestyle.

✓ *Environmental Drivers* are such natural occurrences as droughts or floods, or a recycling initiative.

✓ *Government Drivers* usually involve deregulation or regulation, but also may be the passage of a major law or change in legislation that has a direct impact on the organization's business. One such example was the challenge to Microsoft when it tried to purchase Intuit Software.

✓ *Public Perception Drivers* are propelled by such things as media or image making or breaking circumstances. For example, a scandal or misconception may force the business to enact a strategy and allocate resources to change the way business is done. The scandal within United Way a few years ago is an example of a Public Perception Driver.

✓ *Market/Product Drivers* are new products, services, or competitors that force an organization to change strategies or support. An example of a Product Driver is the decision of Coca Cola to "change its formula" only to determine its consumers, in many cases, preferred Coke "Classic."

✓ *Change in System, Process, or Key Policy Drivers* are new systems or major conversions that affect employees, customers, and the manner in which the company does business.

✓ *Customer Drivers* are usually perceptions or things customers influence that cause organizations to react. A Customer Driver may occur as a result of a change in the marketplace or it may arise as a response to specific customer reactions (such as when customers boycotted canned tuna because dolphins were caught in tuna nets).

✓ *Shareholder or Financial Drivers* are usually based on the perceptions of Wall Street or shareholders. A Financial Driver may be driven by banks or other financial institutions. In the mid-1980's banks were very reluctant to grant loans to car manufacturers, thus changing the manner in which General Motors and Ford were able to compete and do business.

Linking Business Drivers and Performance Needs to Evaluation

With a clear understanding of the Performance Need, the Business Drivers, and how they impact the organization, you are ready to determine the "level(s)" of evaluation that will most appropriately measure the effectiveness of the solution. These levels of evaluation are also referred to as the "Balanced Scorecard" and include the following:

✓ *Customer Perspective:* Did the program meet the need or expectation? Was it delivered using the right method at a time when it was needed? Are the users or customers satisfied with the "end product"?

✓ *Learning Perspective:* Did the participants gain skills or knowledge that they did not have before? Has there been an improvement in the methods they use? Can we measure the difference (pre/posttest or baseline)?

✓ *Business Perspective:* Has there been an impact "back on the job" as a result of the intervention or program? Has productivity increased? Is job behavior different? Have costs decreased? Is technology being used where it was not before? Are we getting the results back on the job as we had planned?

✓ *Financial Perspective:* Did the program have a financial payoff or benefit to the company? Did the program assist in increasing revenue, decreasing costs, or provide some type of return-on-investment (ROI) or financial impact?

The Business Driver, and ultimately the Performance Need, indicate which level(s) of evaluation will be the most efficient and effective for the organization to pursue in determining the intervention's impact. For example:

If the Business Driver Is:	*The Level(s) of Evaluation Would Be:*
Human Resource Drivers	Customer Perspective, Learning Perspective, Business Perspective
Change in System, Policy Drivers	Customer Perspective, Learning Perspective, Business Perspective
Market/Product Drivers	Customer Perspective
Public Perception Drivers	Customer Perspective
Economic Drivers	Financial Perspective

The Balanced Scorecard and
Kirkpatrick's Four Levels of Evaluation

These four levels of evaluation may look familiar as they are based on Kirkpatrick's four levels of training evaluation and a "balanced scorecard" approach. For example:

Perspective/Scorecard	*Level of Evaluation*
Customer Perspective: Did the participants gain information they needed or expected from the program? Do they believe they will be able to use it back on the job? Was it delivered in the right method at a time when it was needed?	LEVEL 1— Reaction
Learning Perspective: Did the participants gain skills or knowledge that they did not have before? Has there been an improvement in the methods they use? Can we measure the difference (pre/posttest or baseline)?	LEVEL 2— Learning
Business Perspective: Has the participant transferred what was learned back to the job? Have business or productivity increased? Is job behavior different? Have processes or costs improved? Is technology being used where it was not before? Are we getting the results back on the job as we had planned?	LEVEL 3— Transfer
Financial Perspective: Did the program have a financial payoff or benefit to the company? Did the program assist in increasing revenue, decreasing costs, or providing some type of return-on-investment (ROI)?	LEVEL 4— ROI

The need for training evaluation must be clearly linked to the business strategy that drives the need for performance improvement. Training and performance interventions often fail because they are not integrated with the business strategy, thus causing the solution to fall short of the real performance need.

Evaluation, especially at Level 3 (Behavior or Transfer) and Level 4 (ROI), is frequently seen as too difficult to conduct. In truth, if your training or performance intervention has been linked to the business strategy, the results and the contribution of the training or intervention will be apparent to you.

By understanding the business strategy (the Balanced Scorecard) you will be able to select the correct level of evaluation (Kirkpatrick's four levels) and provide meaningful evaluation results that are easily understood and embraced by your clients.

Training organizations that have adopted this method of evaluation have successfully demonstrated training's link to the organization's overall business strategy and, as a result, have increased their credibility, demand, and resources. This linkage is imperative if performance improvement interventions are to be taken seriously and viewed as powerful business strategies.

REFERENCES

Brinkerhoff, R.O. (1987) *Achieving Results from Training*. San Francisco: Jossey-Bass.

Burns, W., Ed. (1992) *Performance Measurement, Evaluation, and Incentives*. Boston: Harvard Business School Press.

Kaplan, R., and Norton, D. *The Balanced Scorecard–Measures that Drive Performance*. Harvard Business Review, January-February 1992.

Kaplan, R., and Norton, D. *Putting the Balanced Scorecard to Work*. Harvard Business Review, September-October 1993.

Kaplan, R., and Norton, D. *Using the Balanced Scorecard as a Strategic Management System*. Harvard Business Review, January-February 1996.

Kirkpatrick, D. (1994) *Evaluating Training Programs–The Four Levels*. San Francisco: Berrett-Koehler.

Phillips, J., Ed. (1994) *Measuring Return on Investment*. Alexandria: ASTD Press.

Robinson, D. and Robinson, J. (1989) *Training for Impact*. San Francisco: Jossey-Bass.

About the Editors

Mel Silberman, Ph.D. is President of Active Training (26 Linden Lane, Princeton, New Jersey 08540, 609-924-8157, mel@tigger.jvnc.net, http:\\www.activetraining.com). He is also Professor of Adult and Organizational Development at Temple University where he specializes in instructional design and team building.

He is the author of

> *Active Training* (Lexington Books, 1990)
> *101 Ways to Make Training Active* (Pfeiffer & Co., 1995)
> *Active Learning* (Allyn & Bacon, 1996)

He is the editor of:

> *20 Active Training Programs,* vol. I (Pfeiffer & Co., 1992)
> *20 Active Training Programs,* vol. II (Pfeiffer & Co., 1994)
> *20 Active Training Programs,* vol. III (Pfeiffer & Co., 1997)
> *The 1996 McGraw-Hill Training and Performance*
>   *Sourcebook*
> *The 1996 McGraw-Hill Team and Organization*
>   *Development Sourcebook*

Mel has consulted for hundreds of corporate, governmental, educational, and human service organizations worldwide. His recent clients include:

AT&T International	Midlantic Bank
Merrill Lynch	Texas Instruments
Automated Data Processing	Meridian Bank
Bristol Myers-Squibb	Franklin Quest
Devereux Foundation	J. P. Morgan, Inc.
Hoffman-LaRoche	U.S. Army
Bell Atlantic	Hospital of the University of PA
ARCO Chemical	Penn State University

He is also a popular speaker at professional conferences.

Carol Auerbach is an independent management consultant (609 Kingston Rd., Baltimore, MD 21212, 410-377-9257, cauerbach@aol.com). A former trainer for Mellon Bank and CIGNA Corporation, she now designs and conducts training on a wide variety of topics. Carol collaborated with Mel previously on *Active Training* and served as the assistant editor of *The 1996 McGraw-Hill Training and Performance Sourcebook* and *The 1996 McGraw-Hill Team and Organization Development Sourcebook.*

Are you interested in being a contributor to *The 1998 McGraw-Hill Training and Performance Sourcebook?*

In the course of your professional work, you have probably developed exercises, handouts, instruments, short articles, and other printed materials that could be useful to a wide audience of consultants, trainers, and performance specialists. Consider your favorite piece of work for publication. The *1998 Sourcebook* will contain another 40 practical tools to improve learning and performance. Would you like to contribute one of them? Join our impressive list of contributors.

For more information, contact:

Mel Silberman, Editor
The McGraw-Hill Training and Performance Sourcebook
c/o Active Training
26 Linden Lane
Princeton, NJ 08540
609-924-8157
609-924-4250 fax
mel@tigger.jvnc.net